PAYMENT IN FULL

PAYMENT IN FULL

A GUIDE TO SUCCESSFUL BILL COLLECTING

By Leonard Bendell

TRIAD PUBLISHING COMPANY   GAINESVILLE, FLORIDA

Printed in the United States of America

Published and distributed by
Triad Publishing Company, Inc.
1110 Northwest Eighth Avenue
Gainesville, Florida 32601

The Collection Call, companion video dramatizations based on
Payment In Full, is also available from Triad.

Library of Congress Cataloging-in-Publication Data
Bendell, Leonard, 1941-
    Payment in full.
    1. Collecting of accounts.   I. Title.
HG3752.5.B45   1987   658.8'8   87-10769
ISBN 0-937404-05-5

The laws that are noted in this book may or may not apply to your situation. However, the suggested procedures, if followed, shall provide you with an ethical, legal, and moral approach to the collection of past-due accounts receivable.

The material given in this book is general in nature and does not consitute legal advice. It is highly recommended that any policies you establish be reviewed by your legal council before implimentation. No policy or procedure suggested should replace advice of your own legal council.

CONTENTS

Introduction, 7

PART I: IT'S YOUR MONEY!
1. Your Goal: Payment In Full, 11
2. Identifying Delinquent Accounts, 15
3. What Is Your Company Policy?, 19

PART II: PLANNING FOR SUCCESS
1. Know Your Debtors, 43
2. Develop the Basic Skills, 51
3. Be Informed, 59
4. Finding Missing Debtors: Skiptracing, 61

PART III: THE COLLECTION CALL
1. The Opening, 73
2. The Body of the Call, 75
3. Finding the Solution, 87
4. Motivating the Debtor, 93
5. Overcoming Objections, 105
6. The Close, 113
7. Sample Collection Calls, 115
8. Mistakes of Beginning Collector, 129

CONTENTS

PART IV: SELECTING A PROFESSIONAL COLLECTION
SERVICE, 131

PART V: COLLECTING WITHIN GOVERNMENT
GUIDELINES
1. Why Credit Grantors Have to Be Careful, 141
2. Legal Use of Telephone for Debt Collecion, 143
3. Questions Answered About the FDCPA, 155

Standard Collections Office Abbreviations, 169

SAMPLES AND GUIDES

Aging Sample, 17
Invoice Sample, 26
Steps in the Collection Effort, 29
Collection Letter Samples, 31-35
Average Debtor Expenses, 44
Positive Benefits of Paying, 70
Collection Call Sequence, 72
Telephone Do's and Don'ts, 86
ABCs of Telephone Collecting, 91
Motivating Sentences That Collect, 104
FCC Notice: Use of Telephone
   for Debt Collection Purposes, 144

INTRODUCTION

ARE YOU A CREDITOR? If so, you may also be a debt collector. Many people employed in such diverse occupations as law, medicine, and insurance, or in other service fields may not think of themselves in that role. But, if you provide goods or services and accept anything other than full and immediate payment, you are a credit grantor, or creditor. As such, you may well have debtors, which means that you, or someone in your firm, will be a collector.

Bad debt is a growing problem. A recent survey by Money magazine found that in 1986 the average amount owed increased to $40,500, from $33,300 the year before — an increase of nearly twenty-two percent.

In 1985, over five million accounts "skipped" without paying as promised. More than 13.8 billion dollars in unpaid accounts were turned over to collection agencies. Private individuals and credit grantors not employing collection agencies also lost many millions of dollars. As a result, every man, woman, and child in the United States had to pay $76.00 *extra* for all the things they purchased, just to cover the bad debts of those who didn't pay as promised!

Is there anything you can do to reduce your exposure to bad debt and keep your losses to a minimum? Definitely, yes! Only about three percent of the debtor population are deliberate credit criminals — the ones who never intended to pay for what they received. Ninety-seven percent of your delinquent accounts intended to pay the bill, and most will still pay if they are properly motivated to do so. But it takes learning what will motivate them, and sometimes it takes creative solutions to their financial problems.

A collector has three basic goals: to obtain payment in accordance with the terms, maintain good will, and keep credit losses to a minimum. The purpose of this book is to show you how to achieve these goals.

Payment In Full will teach you skills and techniques that will help you collect what you are owed. You will learn how to communicate with debtors, classify them, categorize the reasons they haven't paid, counteract excuses, and motivate them so they will want to pay. You will learn about collection and credit policies, how to turn negatives into positives, and how to turn bad debt into good money.

You will be able to obtain a greater number of Payments In Full. You will also help reduce the high cost of bad credit.

PART I

IT'S YOUR MONEY!

1. YOUR GOAL: PAYMENT IN FULL

Everybody owes money.
The ones who don't pay are your target.

REGARDING YOUR DELINQUENT accounts, you have one objective, which is to obtain Payment In Full as soon as possible. A corollary is that you want to go about it legitimately and in the least offensive manner.

Receiving the entire amount owed is called Payment In Full, which is known in the collection industry as "PIF" and sometimes written P/I/F. Receiving PIF is called "getting PIFed."

When you are collecting a delinquent account, PIF need not be the immediate receipt of cash, check, or money order. *PIF occurs either when you receive the money or when you get the debtor to agree to terms that are reasonable, that you feel he or she can keep.* If the debtor makes a promises to pay and you accept that promise, your call or letter has achieved its purpose.

Let's say your debtor comes in and says, *"Yes, I owe you the $500. I can't pay you a dime right now, but in thirty days I can pay you all $500."*

You say, *"If there is no other alternative we'll hold off for thirty days."*

Haven't you achieved Payment In Full? From the collector's point of view there is nothing more you can do with that account until thirty days have passed and the payment is due. You don't want to talk to the debtor again next week. You might call on the day that the money is due, just as a reminder. But you're not going to do anything else in-between.

So, for your purposes, you achieve PIF when you make an agreement. It does not make any difference what the terms are — whether it's $10 a week or $500 in thirty days. Once you and the debtor agree to terms, there is nothing more that you can do but wait and see if the promise is kept. As long as the debtor continues with that agreement, you are achieving your terms. To the best of your knowledge, your call has secured PIF.

BENEFITS OF EARLY PIF

You need to obtain Payment In Full as soon as possible because the cost of collecting the account increases with every day it remains uncollected. Each time an account is handled there are administrative costs, collection costs, and overhead costs, and these continue until the account is finally paid or closed. Every contact that is made and each payment that is processed costs money.

The following all add to the expense of processing delinquent accounts: setting up the collections file, skiptracing, sending statements, writing letters, making telephone calls, keeping notes and records, and preparing status reports.

Conservative estimates place the cost of sending statements at $1.00 each, with each follow-up letter at $1.50. These figures do not include what you pay for postage, stuffing envelopes, or zip code separation. The average office that sends three statements and three collection letters spends about $10 per account.

12

There is another reason for obtaining PIF as soon as you can: the longer a delinquent account is held, the lower its chances of being collected at all.

Up to thirty days past due is your prime collection period, and collecting on the first contact will, of course, give you the maximum chance of return. Most efforts take place during the period between thirty and ninety days past due. Beyond ninety days, there is little reason to continue because recovery percentages drop dramatically. And I don't mean your recovery will drop ten percent or fifteen percent, it will drop by eighty percent!

The collection industry has a saying, "Time is the debtor's safe refuge." If an individual owes the money today, ninety days from now he's barely going to remember why he owed it. And even if he does remember that he had medical tests or his windows washed, the benefit is long gone, and he has little interest in spending money out of current income for something he perceives as having no present benefit. So, the longer you wait, the less likely he will respond.

2 . IDENTIFYING DELINQUENT ACCOUNTS

COLLECTORS' LAW
No one is completely honest.
Honesty has variables that change with the degree of pressure.
Temptation is the seed of dishonesty.
Financial pressure is the seed of need.

AS A COLLECTOR trying to obtain Payment In Full, you want to move each debtor through the decision-making process toward what you want him to do. What you want him to do, simply, is to pay what he owes, to live up to the terms of the original agreement.

Doctor Kindly and Mrs. Patient made an agreement: The doctor agreed to remove Susan Patient's tonsils and Mrs. Patient agreed to pay the doctor $500 after the operation.

Community Roofing Company and Mr. Leaky made an agreement: Community Roofing agreed to replace Mr. Leaky's roof and Mr. Leaky agreed to pay the company $5,000, at the rate of $500 per month.

Transactions like these are so commonplace that you may not think of them in the same way you would a contract. That is, not until the party who has agreed to pay starts to need additional prodding. But, how do you know the correct point to begin that prodding? What is your method of identifying delinquencies and for finding out just how late they are?

ACCOUNTS RECEIVABLE AGING

Account aging is the method by which you can track the debts that are delinquent. It is the fundamental tool for tracking potential collection problems. Properly utilized, it will aid greatly in meeting your collection goals.

An aging lists all the accounts owed to you and tells you their status. In other words, it shows the length of time each account has been in the house and whether or not it is in accordance with your terms or is now beyond the terms.

You can think of an aging as reflecting the three W's of collections:

Who: the party(ies) owing.
What: the amount owed.
When: how long ago (in days) was payment due.

Understanding what an aging is and how it works is important not only for identifying delinquencies, but also because it contains the information you need for making a collection call. You must know: How old is the account? Why are you getting this account to collect? What has the debtor not done that he or she agreed to do? What are the terms?

If you do not already use an aging receivable list, this would be a good time to begin. Take an accounting ledger sheet and list your customers' names down the left hand side. Make several columns and across the top label the columns, "Current," "31 - 60 days," "61 - 90 days," "Over 90 days," "Total." Most agings do not extend beyond 180 days, which is six months. Accounts over six months are usually removed from the receivables and sent to a third party collector. Enter the amounts owed by each debtor in the appropriate column. As each account is paid, simply cross it out. Then weekly or monthly, add up the amounts owed by each account (across) and add the columns (vertically). Both totals should be the same. Then start a new sheet with the new and remaining accounts in their appropriate columns. Most offices update on a monthly basis when they do their monthly statements.

All accounts are delinquent when they have not been paid in accordance with your terms. If your terms state that payment is due in thirty days, accounts in the 31 - 60 days column are delinquent. The ones that begin to appear in the 61 days and beyond columns are the most likely to become bad debts if proper collection steps are not followed.

SAMPLE AGING

CUSTOMER	CURRENT	31-60	61-90	OVER 90	TOTAL
C. Benson		25.00			25.00
George Lee	15.00	40.00			55.00
Bill Edison				115.10	115.10
Sharon Green			76.50	76.50	
Sam Hall			45.00	45.00	
	15.00	65.00	121.50	115.10	316.60

It is important to remember that the "current" column contains amounts that could have been charged at any time during the statement period, from one to twenty-nine days. Therefore, an account that has received two statements thirty days apart could be as young as thirty-one days from the charge or as old as fifty-nine days. An aging list is simply a guide, showing the accounts on a statement to statement basis.

3. WHAT IS YOUR COMPANY POLICY?

*A wise dentist collects his fee
while the patient's tooth is still aching.*
(Ancient Chinese saying)

BEFORE YOU CAN BEGIN any collection effort, you need to have a policy for credit and collections. A policy includes pre-defined guidelines for granting credit and a procedure to follow after you have discovered that somebody is late in paying your bill. A policy tells you what to do, when to do it, and how to do it. Whether its approach is strict, medium, or lenient reflects the philosophy of your office toward the collection of bad debt.

KINDS OF POLICIES

If you sell goods or services on credit you already have a policy, whether you are aware of it or not. When this policy has not been formally stated, it is likely to be a subjective policy, meaning that decisions are made on a case-by-case basis by management or by the person doing the collecting. An objective policy is one that is written down and applied to everyone in the same way.

A SUBJECTIVE POLICY

Subjectivity is a poor management technique because it leaves each decision up to the collector. It is more likely to create collection problems than solve them, for the following reasons:
1. Relates to the person, not the credit problem.
2. Tends not to be uniformly applied; is too flexible with too many variables.
3. Is too easily changed.
4. Is not fair to other debtors.
5. Provides the collector with nothing to fall back on when confronted by the debtor. You are not able to say, for example, "I don't have the authority to do that," because you *can* do whatever you want.

AN OBJECTIVE POLICY

The most effective kind of company policy is an objective one, because it consists of a method and procedure *in writing* that responds to a set of circumstances. An objective policy:
1. Relates to the credit situation itself rather than to the individual.
2. Provides for uniformity in the decision-making process. The rules are the same for everyone, and they are applied in the same way to everyone.
3. Provides office staff with guidelines they can depend on.
4. Provides a step-by-step chain responding to circumstances.
5. Is fair to all.
6. Assures management that its personnel are educated in the principles of the company.
7. Reduces costs by eliminating time lost in making decisions (and reduces losses by "skips" because the policy describes when to stop wasting time on uncollectable debts).
8. Allows eventual third party action to become contiguous and complimentary to the in-house program.

THE BEST POLICY

A comprehensive policy supported by detailed procedures helps control delinquencies because it lets everyone you deal with know what to expect. Your customers are more likely to give your office higher priority when it comes time to pay their bills when they know you take action against credit offenders.

When the rules are written down, your staff has the opportunity to be empathetic with the debtor ("It's not *my* policy, it's the *office's* policy") while at the same time maintaining a firm stance regarding the urgency of the payment.

Every employee learns what the policy is and how to implement it. But—and this is one of the most important parts of any policy—everyone has to follow it. There should be enough flexibility in the policy to cover different situations, but breakdowns in the policy itself must not be allowed. Management, especially, must not intercede and stretch the rules, or the collection effort will be undermined.

The Slowpay family had owed Dr. Wellness $750 for over six months. After many attempts to communicate with the family, the office manager finally found them and convinced them to come into the office.

Mr. Slowpay initially claimed that he was not able to make any payments. However, after being shown the results of investigation—that it was known that both husband and wife were gainfully employed, with the ability to pay the account and probably in only two or three payments—he agreed to pay the full amount in three equal installments over a ninety-day period.

Then, Mr. Slowpay went home and called Dr. Wellness with the plea that he was not capable of making the payments he had agreed to. The doctor told Mr. Slowpay it would be all right to spread the payments out over many more months. When the office manager later explained to him that the family did indeed have

21

the ability to pay as Mr. Slowpay had agreed, the doctor was sorry he had become involved, but he had already made a commitment for the extended time.

The moral of the story is that you must not override the people who work for you until you have all the facts.

WHAT A POLICY SHOULD INCLUDE

Your company policy should cover every step in the decision-making process regarding granting credit and making collections, from establishing the frequency with which statements and collections messages are sent, to handling bad debts. The following kinds of information should be incorporated into your policy.

TO WHOM DO YOU GIVE CREDIT?

You might give credit only after running a credit check. Or only after someone has been your customer for one year or more. Or only to those who fill out your your information form satisfactorily (you might be cautious in extending credit to someone who has moved several times in the past year). The decision is up to you, but once you have defined how credit is given, you must not make exceptions.

Doctor Efficient has a sign in the waiting room that states that all accounts must be paid before leaving the office. Mrs. Pretty is a new patient, nicely dressed. After her check-up she tells the office manager that she's terribly sorry but she just doesn't seem to have her checkbook with her today. The office manager is busy and hasn't noticed that Mrs. Pretty didn't finish filling out the information form — she omitted giving her place of employment, person responsible for the bills, her insurance company, and the name of a relative not living at her address.

"That's OK," the office manager says. "Just mail us a check when you get home."

The bill is now four months past due, and the office manager is having a hard time finding Mrs. Pretty.

The doctor had not intended to grant credit to Mrs. Pretty, a stranger, and this was clearly stated on the sign; however, once she received treatment there was no way to undo it. *The doctor had unwittingly extended credit to her!* The best defense against non-payment at this point is to be sure to have enough facts about the patient to collect from her.

HOW MUCH CREDIT DO YOU GIVE?

Once you have decided to extend credit to someone, is the amount unlimited? How do you establish credit limits? Make your guidelines part of your written policy so no one in your office has to make a subjective decision when someone new walks in the door.

WHAT INFORMATION DO YOU REQUIRE?

You should try to get as much information as you can on each new patient, client, or customer *before* the goods or services are given. Not only will you be able to evaluate a person as a credit risk, the more you know, the easier it will be to discuss an overdue bill or, if necessary, locate a debtor.

This is rarely done, however. Retailers are more concerned with the sale, medical offices with their patients, and others with their service or product. They don't recognize the need for this information until a payment is past due. And by then it usually is too late.

The following is, of course, an exaggeration, but

think how frustrating it would be if you were trying
to collect $3,000 or $4,000, and you went to the file
and found: Name, John Doe. Address, unknown.
Phone number, unknown. Workplace, unknown.

The easiest time to gather the information you need is at the
beginning of each individual's credit life with your office. Many
health and medical facilities, the credit offices of department
stores, and others routinely hand each new patient or customer a
form to fill out requesting name, address, place of work, person
responsible for debt, name, address, and telephone number of a
relative living at a different address, etc.

If the obtaining of such information is part of your policy,
then you should also include the next step. Does someone check
each form for legible handwriting and completeness? What if
some spaces are left blank (perhaps the individual doesn't know
all the answers)?

The following is basic information to have on hand:

1. Complete and accurate name of the debtor. (If a married
   woman, include maiden name.)
2. Present or last known address (and any other addresses
   known).
3. Marital status. If married, complete and accurate name of
   spouse (former if divorced).
4. Approximate age of debtor (and also of spouse).
5. Employer and employment of debtor (and also of spouse).
6. If a company, its legal status. Determine whether you are
   dealing with a sole proprietor, corporation, partnership, etc.

Some of a person's identifying factors are easily changeable;
others are difficult to change. The following are relatively constant, and should be obtained:

1. Driver's license number and state of issue. (Make a photo-
   copy if possible.)
2. Social security number.
3. Date of birth.

4. Any readily identifying marks.
5. If applicable: Insurance company policy number, name of insured, type of policy (group, personal, etc.).

Any time you ask information of people, you must be careful not to invade anyone's privacy, or exceed the boundaries of what is legal, moral, and ethical.

WRONG PARTY

One of the most frequent problems in debt collection is the lack of sufficient data to positively identify who owes you money. I have seen many accounts that had to be closed because certain information was not available. If the debtor states the debt is not his by virtue of his being the wrong party, the burden is upon you to prove he is the correct party. Moreover, when your collection policy includes forwarding the account to a third party (collection agency, attorney, court system), it becomes incumbent upon you to provide information that will alleviate the objection of wrong party claim, and simultaneously eliminate legal or potential legal liability from wrongful prosecution.

WHAT ARE YOUR TERMS?

Does your customer/patient/client owe the money when the service is rendered or product is received? When the bill (invoice) is received? Thirty days after the invoice date? In other words, what are your terms? These terms should be clearly stated on the invoice, e.g., *Net due upon receipt* or *Net 30 days*. Other

PRODUCTIONS

INVOICE

Date February 19, 1987

Name John D. Doe

Invoice # 00141

Address Rt. 1, Box 984

Terms Net Upon Delivery

Anywhere, USA 00000

Charge C O D

Folio # 842 Description See Below

2 hours editing time @ $175.00	$350.00
4 dubs @ $25.00	100.00
4 3/4" videotapes @ $20.00	80.00
	$530.00

Sub Total	$530.00
Tax	4.00
Grand Total	$534.00

PAYABLE TO: PENGUIN PRODUCTIONS

P.O. Box 76128
Ocala, Florida 32676   (904) 854-6000

10461 S.W. Hwy. 484
Dunnellon, Florida 32630

credit conditions to establish, if applicable, are interest rate charged and at what time, and any late penalties.

Sometimes, in order to collect an account, you may agree to change the terms. For example, you might agree that instead of your stated terms of "net due upon receipt" you will allow this person to pay half the money in thirty days and the balance in sixty days.

> Mrs. Invalid has been in the hospital, and the bill is $1000. The insurance pays $800, and there's a $200 balance. When is that $200 due? If the hospital's policy is that payments are due when the patient checks out, the $200 is due now. But Mrs. Invalid doesn't have the money. She says to the patient counselor, "I can pay you in ten days," and she is told, "OK, ten days is fine."
>
> Ten days pass and she still hasn't paid. When was she late? Was she late from the day she walked out of the hospital or was she late at ten days? The answer is, she was late at ten days. The reason is that the hospital *agreed to new terms*.

Although you may agree to new terms when there is a reason, you should *never offer them*. Giving terms is the same as making a loan to the debtor.

INVOICE

The invoice is usually presented at the time services are rendered, though some offices mail them later. The invoice should clearly state the terms of sale, as well as interest charges and late penalties. If the terms are "net 30 days," the invoice should state whether you expect payment thirty days from delivery/service date or thirty days from invoice date.

27

STATEMENT

The statement is sent at a specified interval after the invoice. My suggestion is that you send the statement two weeks after the date the invoice is due.

Many offices send a statement at the end of the month, regardless which day of the month the account was due. This may be easier, but it means that some people receive statements a few days after the transaction and others receive them almost a month afterwards. You will have better control of your accounts by sending the statement at a set time after the invoice.

I recommend that you send a statement only once. You must assume that the individual knows he owes the money. He is entitled to one statement. After that *he is late* and should be treated accordingly. Experience shows that constantly sending statements is of little value.

It's a good idea to print or stamp "Address Correction Requested" on the envelope that holds the first statement. Doing this will automatically let you know when people have had an address change (if they have left a forwarding address with the post office). The postal service has a small charge for each correction.

LATE NOTICE

You must tell the individual he is late by sending him a late notice, which is also a form of statement. Send it two weeks after the statement. I believe that it is a waste of time to send more than one late notice. But if you decide to use a second notice, send it one month after the first one.

It is appropriate for the first late notice to be a copy of the statement with a sticker or rubber stamped message added, such as *Past Due - Please Remit*. If you use a second late notice, you may wish to add a stronger message, to the effect that *Unless you contact this office within 10 days, this account will be referred for collection*. This cannot be an idle threat, however; if you say you will refer for collection, you must do it.

28

Some offices have had success with short handwritten notes on the statement or signing a name after the standard message. It is possible that the debtor perceives more of a threat from a "real person" than from an impersonal stickered or rubber-stamped message.

STEPS IN THE COLLECTION EFFORT

TIME FROM PURCHASE/SERVICE	*WHAT TO DO*
Same day	Invoice
2 weeks later	Statement
30 days delinquent	1st late notice
60 days delinquent	2nd late notice
75 days delinquent	1st phone call (or 3rd late notice)
90 days delinquent	Decision time *(keep in house longer, close, or refer to third party)*

COLLECTION LETTER

I prefer to omit the collection letter and go directly to the telephone call. However, there are reasons that many collectors use them. The available staff for making calls may be too limited to telephone every overdue account. Or the calls may have to be long distance, and some accounts do not involve large enough sums to warrant the expense.

Your policy should specify when and under what circumstances collection letters are sent. Keep them short and to the point. Use the following guidelines for more effective letters:

1.   Be brief.

2.   Be specific. Tell how much is owed, how much is past due, how long past due, and what is the debt for (merchandise? service?).

3.   Use short sentences and simple words. Use words and phrases that cannot possibly be misunderstood.

4.   Tell why you are writing. *"Your account is 60 days overdue."*

5.   Tell what you want debtor to do. *"Please bring in a check by 5 o'clock tomorrow."*

6.   Encourage the debtor to respond to you. Ask questions like: *"Why haven't you paid?" "Did you forget us?" "Is there a misunderstanding?"*

7.   Do not use colored paper. You don't want your letters to look like the dunning form letters that debtors are already familiar with. These tend to be tossed in the wastebasket unopened.

8.   Do not use cheap paper. Higher quality paper will make it appear that the account is important, which means that you are more likely to pursue collection efforts.

9.   Do not make threats. A threat is something you say you will do, but never intend to do. You may not even be capable of doing it. For example, never threaten someone's credit rating unless you are a member of a credit bureau and place your delinquent accounts in their records as a regular practice.

It is extremely important that you do not place yourself in the position of doing *anything* that can be considered a threat. Therefore, if you write in a collection letter that "Unless you contact this office within 10 days we will refer this account to our attorney for collection," or "We will refer this account for suit," you must be prepared to refer it to the appropriate individual or attorney for that action.

In the case of suit, you also must be able to demonstrate, first, that this is your policy and second, that you normally follow that policy. There are times when an unsuccessful collection effort leads to a lawsuit. If the debtor finds an attorney (or legal aid society) to help him, one of the first things that attorney will attempt to do is discredit your actions by claiming harrassment or threats. *Any time you say you are going to sue in ten days and don't, or say you will refer for suit in ten days and don't, you can be leaving yourself open for legal action.*

10. Do not give deadlines unless you are sure that you can follow them. You have to be able to take the action you say will be taken when the deadline is reached.

11. If you can do so legally, leave the debtor with a word picture so that he understands what can happen to him: *"Mr. Debtor, we know that you do not want to hurt your credit rating."* (But that comment should only be used if you actually report to a credit agency or credit bureau.)

12. If you send several statements and letters, use a prescribed sequence, by degree of default.

31

Drs. Jones, Smith and Brown
1909 Harris Blvd.
Suite 101
Blackburg, Anywhere

May 20, 1986

RE: Balance Due - $271.49

Dear Mr. Richardson,

As you know, medical expenses are due at time of service. We made an exception in your case because it was an emergency and you were not prepared to make payment at that time.

However, it has been six weeks and we have not received any payment on account.

We know of your outstanding reputation in this town and are sure that you would not want to jeopardize it by continuing to leave this charge unpaid.

Please remit immediately to the above address, attention to Ms. Connie James. We will hold your file on the cashier's desk until we receive your check.

Thank you for taking care of this matter promptly.

Sincerely,

Connie James,
Cashier

H & M Tire Stores, Inc.
2 South Main Street
Middleburg, USA 00000

February 2, 1987

RE: Balance owed on tire purchase--$213.00

Dear Mrs.Smith,

   As you know,your account is seriously
past due.

   It will be in your best interest to mail
or bring to our store a check for the balance within the week.

   This will put your account back in good
standing and enable us to give a good
recommendation should anyone inquire about
your credit standing with our company.

   Thank you for giving this matter your
immediate attention.

                    Sincerely,

                    John Anderson
                    Credit Manager

Sylvan's Department Store
174 Main Street
Anywhere, USA 00000

January 19, 1987

Mr. Charles Wallace
P.O. Box 6702
Swansea, N. Dakota 00000

RE: Balance Due - $92.56

Dear Mr. Wallace,

   This letter is to remind you that all purchases at Sylvan's are due and payable in full
at the end of each month.

   Interest is added onto any account that
goes past the due date without being paid.

   We ask you to please remit the entire above
balance in full within the next 5 days to
avoid both the interest being added and your
credit rating with us falling to an undesir-
able level.

   We expect to have your check in this office
within 5 days.

   Thank you for your immediate cooperation.

Sincerely,

John Doe
Credit Manager

Style Department Store
2219 Front Street
Uptown, America 12345

April 5, 1987

<u>FINAL NOTICE</u>

Mrs. Emma J. Stone
3270 S. Park Street
Uptown, USA 12346

RE: Balance Due - $314.70

Dear Mrs. Stone:

   This is the third and last time that we will bill
you for your purchases at our store. Your account is
seriously past due and must be paid now.

   When you opened your account with us, it was understood that payment would be made promptly. However,
you have not lived up to that understanding.

   Please send or bring in your check or money order
within the next five days or further action will have
to be taken to collect the money owed to us.

Sincerely,

John T. Abernathy
Credit Manager

Roland W. Wilson, DDS
#11 Medical Arts Building
Overview, USA 10011

December 8, 1986

Mrs. Gertrude L. Smith
Rt. 1, Box 56
Overview, USA 10012

RE: $191.00

Dear Mrs. Smith:

   Your account with this office is so far past due
that we are going to have to take serious steps to
collect the money you owe us.

   Please mail or bring in your payment in full
within five days. If we do not receive it in that
time period, we will be forced to turn this over to a
professional for collection.

   Thank you for your prompt attention to this
matter.

Sincerely,

Jane Jones
Office Manager

COLLECTION CALL

The collection call is your best tool for collecting delinquent accounts. It is the best and usually only way you will find out why payment hasn't been made. Where a letter may be easy to ignore, a phone call demands attention. It provides an immediate response and allows two-way communication. It will allow you to determine whether you can ever expect payment or should stop wasting time on accounts that are uncollectable. Wait no longer than seven days after sending the last written communication to make a phone call to the debtor.

The steps and sequence for collection calls will be covered in Part III.

FINAL ACTION

If you have not collected an account after going through the other steps according to your collections policy, chances are that *any* further effort you expend will result in the costs being higher than what you hope to recover. In addition, each minute you spend on accounts that can't or won't pay is a minute away from accounts that will pay.

Therefore, you have to determine the point in the collection effort when it is unprofitable to continue any further activity. You have to know when to stop. If an account becomes more than ninety days old with no part-payment received and no promise to pay, in most cases it should be referred to a third party. Or, you may decide to close the account if the case is one of hardship or you have decided it will be impossible to collect.

Final action will be one of the following:

1. Close the account with no further action.

2. Refer to collection agency (see Part IV, "Selecting a Professional Collection Service") or your attorney.

3. File a notice with your credit bureau (if you are a member).

Once the credit bureau has been given the information that an individual has not paid the account and/or the account is referred for collection, that information is entered into the debtor's credit record. The next time that individual applies for credit anywhere, the potential creditor can see that he or she has not paid an account. You are responsible that the information is accurate.

Bear in mind that there will be no record as to why the account has not been paid, or even if the referral for collection was just. But it will be there as part of the record until such time in the future that it is cleared up or the statute of limitations expires.

4. Consider filing suit. Remember that every time that you file a lawsuit you have to put up the costs of that lawsuit until you are able to collect the money back. You should be very sure that the debt is legitimate and has not been paid, and that you have done everything within your power to obtain payment on the account.

The size of the claim plays a part in the decision to take a debtor to small claims court. Obviously, with an overdue bill that is $10 or $15 or even $40 or $50, the cost of the time involved does not warrant it. It is also important to know whether the debtor has the ability, either now or potentially later, to pay the account. Generally, claims in excess of $100 are worth consideration if the debtor owns property — a home, for example, or anything that you can file a lien on.

Your collections policy should specify the next course of action and how each decision is made—what it is based on as well as who makes it. After an evaluation of all relevant factors, someone will determine that the account is uncollectable. What happens then is most likely based on the amount of money involved. Usually, top management is consulted for a decision requiring legal action.

BAD CHECKS

There is a significant difference between an NSF (non-sufficient funds) check and a closed account. An NSF check could happen in a number of ways, from the person's knowing there were not enough funds to cover it (which is generally fraud), to simply a cross-deposit. Writing checks on a closed account *is* an intent to defraud.

Here is how one medical clinic's policy deals with returned checks. First, the office manager contacts the patient and notifies him/her that the check has been returned by the bank, and asks the patient if the check may be redeposited (if this is the first time the check has been returned), or asks the patient to come to the business office to pick up the check and pay in cash, certified check, or money order. Notes are made in the patient's record as to the amount of check, date it was returned, and what steps were taken.

In order to successfully prosecute a bad check charge, the person accepting the check must be able to identify (beyond a shadow of a doubt) the person who gave it to him. The first step is to write identifying information on the check itself at the time it is accepted: driver's license, a physical description taken from the driver's license, a credit card number or some other form of identification, and the person's place of employment. In Florida, a rubber stamp containing all the basic information required to satisfy state law can be bought at almost any stationery store.

Most states have similar laws. I suggest you contact either the Better Business Bureau or the State's Attorney's Office in your locality to obtain the rules for accepting checks and prosecuting on bad checks.

BANKRUPTCY

Upon receiving a notice informing the creditors that a debtor is filing for bankruptcy, these are the steps commonly taken:

1. Review the account to determine outstanding balance.

2.   Complete the bankruptcy claim form (if the bankruptcy notice states that assets are available) and send to the appropriate court.

3.   If there are no assets available, note in customers record and write off as a bad debt. If you file the bankruptcy claim form and do not receive all or any of the amount due when the bankruptcy claim is settled, you will still have to write off the account.

LEGAL CONSIDERATIONS

Because the law affects every credit and collection transaction, you may wish to include some specifics in your company policy. Here are some suggestions:

1.   Do not disgrace, ridicule, or belittle the debtor as to race, creed, color, or position in society. Do not state or imply that he is dishonest. Do not use profanity.

2.   Do not harrass the debtor. (You will have to define harrassment according to your state's laws.)

3.   Make all telephone calls during reasonable hours. (Check your state's definition of reasonable hours.)

4.   Do not call a debtor's place of employment unless you have been unable to reach him/her at home. If the debtor or the debtor's employer prohibits the call, do not contact the debtor at work.

5.   Do not make strong demands for payment from persons who are not responsible.

6.   Do not use any false or deceptive representation. (But do not give any information about the debt to a third party.)

7.   Make sure that any action threatened is taken by your company within the period of time specified.

PART II

PLANNING FOR SUCCESS

1. KNOW YOUR DEBTORS

A curious collector is a successful collector.
(Collections Industry Saying)

AS A COLLECTOR, you deal essentially with people, you learn about their problems, and you advise and counsel them in solving their problems. Yet, how much do you actually know about the people you deal with? It's so easy to be negative about the person who is slow to pay or who doesn't pay at all. Before you let negativism become encompassing and affect your abililty to collect from them, learn the importance of understanding consumers as individuals.

THE AVERAGE CONSUMER

Each person who owes you money also owes, statistically, eleven other accounts. He or she is a member of an average family consisting of a husband, a wife, and three children. Two of the children are in school and the other is below school age. They probably live in a rented house. On the average, the husband works full-time and the wife works half-time. Their living expenses, depending on where they live, average about $540 per week.

WHAT ARE THEIR EXPENSES

These are the average expenses of an average family in the southeast. You may find it helpful to develop a budget for the typical debtor family in your own community, using local prices to project what they might spend for each of the following

	WEEK	MONTH
Shelter (rent or payment on home, utilities)	$150	$ 650
Food	100	433
Clothing	25	108
Health (doctor, dentist, glasses, health insurance, etc.)	75	325
Incidentals (entertainment, cigarettes, cosmetics, car expenses, etc.)	100	433
Installment payments (TV, appliances, car, furniture, loans)	75	325
Charity	10	43
Savings or insurance	5	22
TOTAL	$540	$2,339

In spite of their difficult financial picture, you cannot take the position that there is no point in trying to collect from your debtors. Should you feel sorry for them? Not if you are going to help them get out of debt. Instead, you must understand them and find ways of helping them solve their financial problems.

OTHER CONSUMERS

Collection problems are part of consumerism — the term used to describe the everyday buying that people do. Consumers are the people you deal with every day. The people who buy goods and services, the people who get sick, the people who pay their bills, the people who don't pay their bills. In other words, it is us. We are all consumers.

Although most debtors fit the picture of the the "average" consumer, the people who owe money transcend all financial strata. Over the years I have collected against county commissioners, judges, and other important people in the community. They are no different from anybody else. They spend more money than they make, and they can't handle some of the predicaments they get into. They have medical disasters, financial disasters, unemployment. There's no difference. Just because people dress nicely and look clean doesn't mean they are going to pay the bill, any more than those who are down and out on their luck.

DEBTOR TYPES

There are several types of people who are regularly in debt. You've probably seen them all. First are the habitual slow pays — people who every month are paying from ninety days ago. There are the big spenders and poor budgeters, frequently people who have to keep up with "The Joneses," without any idea as to how they will be able to pay for things (the new car *and* the gold necklace). There are the people who tend to be irresponsible toward their employment and family obligations, the people who are unavoidably in debt, the people who are incapable of handling their own problems, the "skips," and, finally, the credit criminals.

With the exception of the deliberate credit criminal who provides false information, *all can be persuaded to pay*. The key is in knowing what form of persuasion to use.

UNDERSTAND WHY YOUR DEBTORS ARE IN DEBT

You are going to sell the debtor on the idea of paying the bill today. To successfully motivate him to do what you want, you must first understand why he is in debt. Understanding the general cause of his delinquency brings you a step closer to understanding him as a person. Conversely, as you learn about the person, you will find out more about the underlying cause of his delinquency, which, we find, will fall into one of three general groupings: circumstantial, intellectual, and emotional.

CIRCUMSTANTIAL CAUSES

Some people find themselves deeply in debt because of circumstances they could not have anticipated and could not control. They contracted for goods and services under prudent conditions, but through disaster, unexpected unemployment, sickness, or personal injury found themselves unable to handle their obligations.

INTELLECTUAL CAUSES

Many adults simply cannot budget their income. Such people fail to keep even the most elementary financial records and have no idea how much money they will have after meeting basic expenses. They handle payment of their accounts in a very haphazard manner because they can't plan or budget. For the most part, these are people who *want* to pay their bills, but they need help in managing their finances.

The problem with individuals who fall into this category is that they need counseling but are not willing to accept it. Therefore you cannot expect to retire the obligation from these individuals in any kind of pattern that will make it an easy collection. It will be hard work to collect from them.

EMOTIONAL CAUSES

People who are *emotionally immature* can find themselves overextended before they know it. Then, unlike reasonable adults who face their problems and make arrangements with their creditors, they often are inclined to bluff their way through. Their behavior may even lead you to suspect they are not honest.

They may try to defend themselves from real or imagined consequences by lying, stalling, arguing, running, or blaming others for their problems. In many ways these debtors are like children. How they protect themselves depends on the threat as they see it and how they have learned to defend themselves as children. They may rationalize to themselves that nobody could have done better. If they believe there is an impending action, they may counter with belligerence, cajoling, argument, or flattery.

Such debtors will respond to the same kinds of treatment a wise and firm parent would use. If you can penetrate their defenses, you often get them to accept your help.

You should learn, too, to recognize the *emotionally disturbed debtor*. This person may abuse credit as a response to confused and distorted needs. Compulsive buyers, for example, may be attempting to gain renewed feelings of security and personal worth.

Frauds and criminals generally have *character defects*. They form no real loyalties to any one person, group, or code. They disregard ordinary standards and respond only when cornered. There isn't much you can do to collect from them.

WHY HASN'T YOUR DEBTOR PAID *THIS* BILL?

People who haven't paid a bill haven't paid it for a specific reason. Money is obviously the problem. But the reason that they don't have money available for this payment has become your problem, and you have to solve that problem. If you understand specifically why they don't have the money available, then you can work with them to make it available. You can help them plan the use of their funds. In other words, you can plan your attack to get the funds you need to retire this obligation.

Therefore, the reason the debt occurred is important. Was the person incapable of handling his money? Was it a medical catastrophe? If you don't understand why the individual got into debt (this particular debt, not his overall debt), then you won't be able to collect the money from him; you won't have the information that enables you to formulate strategies and choose the right motivation for him to come forward. As you talk with a debtor and he tells you why he hasn't paid the bill, you will learn about him by listening to what he says. It will always be for one or more of the following reasons:

BIG SPENDER/POOR BUDGETER

These are the people who just can't manage their money. In most cases, you are dealing with an impulse buyer who has never learned self-denial and who doesn't ever think about how he's going to pay for things. If the next door neighbor gets a big-screen TV, he's got to go out and get a big-screen TV. Most of the time he has little or no savings to fall back on.

UNAVOIDABLY IN DEBT

These are usually nice people who pay their bills, but who, right now, find themselves over their head. The cause may be illness or unemployment, or some kind of catastrophe. You can usually work with them. You simply have to work out a plan that will allow them some time to rebuild themselves. If a serious illness has wiped out their financial resources, then you have to make the decision whether or not they are now medically indigent and whether you should even attempt to collect from them.

GRIEVANCE OR DISPUTE

People who have a legitimate grievance or dispute usually withhold payment until the matter is settled.

STALLER OR HABITUAL SLOW PAY

These people usually juggle income to make whatever payments seem most urgent at the moment. Most of them will use manipulative tactics, which may be anything from the popular "The check is in the mail," to complaints about the merchandise or service.

HARDSHIP CASE

Generally, these are honest people who had every intention of paying the bill; however, it is simply beyond their ability, now or in the future, to be able to retire this obligation. They may be on welfare. It is important to identify this type of individual as quickly as possible. So, look at your checklist. You should have enough information on hand to know something about his income. If you decide that the account is not collectable, don't waste time on it.

Being aware of the categories that debtors fall into is a conceptual convenience that can improve your collection technique, whether you are writing a letter to the debtor, calling him on the phone, or interviewing him in your office.

2. DEVELOP THE BASIC SKILLS

What you say is how they'll pay, and
how you say it is how they'll pay it.
(Collections Industry Saying)

NO DOUBT YOU WOULD like to accomplish Payment In Full every time you make a collection call. As a collector, your tools are your intelligence, your personality, and your telephone. When you call debtors you will use psychological methods to get past the defenses they set up and to motivate them. Before you are ready to pick up the phone, however, you need to develop some skills and techniques.

BE ASSERTIVE

When you communicate with a debtor, you are doing more than exchanging words — you are creating an attitude. With as few words as possible, you are attempting to gain the confidence of the debtor and an attitude of cooperation, of willingness to pay. You want the debtor to discuss intimate financial problems and follow your suggestions in solving them.

Much of the debtor's attitude will be created through your attitude. When your attitude is positive, practically everything you present to the debtor is in a positive tone. Therefore, you must have confidence in your ability to convince the debtor to pay in full or make arrangements to pay. You must believe this so strongly that any deviation from the idea would be unacceptable to you. You are calling to make arrangements that will make it easier for the debtor to take care of this financial responsibility. You want to make it easier for him to say yes and to find the earliest convenient time to pay.

You are a salesperson selling Payment In Full, and one of the key attributes of a good salesperson is a positive attitude. Your only disadvantage is having to go to your "buyer" when you are not wanted. But you also have an advantage in that the buyer is already obligated for the sale. If everything you do is positive and you believe there is no way the debtor is not going to pay, most of the time he'll pay. He'll make an agreement, and he'll keep that agreement.

Most people respond to a positively-phrased question such as, "You're considered to be a responsible person, aren't you, Mrs. Jones?" The immediate response you are looking for is, "Yes, I'm responsible and I want to pay this bill." When a positively-worded approach has not produced results, you may be dealing with someone who is more motivated by negatives. In that case, "You don't want to be known as an irresponsible person, Mrs. Jones" may produce results. Be aware, however, that negative statements can backfire and you could lose the collection. As you become more experienced, you will develop the ability to recognize the proper time to use a negative approach.

Be positive about yourself. How you feel about your own abilities will affect the outcome of your calls. You must have confidence in your ability to collect the account. You must be confident that you can control the conversation and that you can convince the debtor that it is to his or her advantage to pay immediately.

You will gain confidence by familiarizing yourself with state and national laws. You should be on very firm ground when you talk to debtors, and know which laws apply to your situation and which do not. For example, in some states, firms are only allowed one contact per month with a debtor.

Be positive about the debtor. You must not consider all debtors as deadbeats or credit criminals, because they are not. You have to keep in mind that most of the people that you deal with are in a situation in which they are financially unable to handle their debts. But most of them are good, honest people, and they do want to pay their bills.

Be positive about your employer. It can be very debilitating to listen to everybody's defenses, objections, and problems all day long, and still feel just just as good on the hundredth phone call of the day as the first phone call. Nevertheless, the image you project over the telephone is extremely important. On this image also rides the reputation and good will of your office.

If you don't believe your company is just in the way it does business, you will have a tough time convincing the debtor that the bill is just. You must also believe that this particular claim is justified and that it should and will be paid. If you have any doubts about the the original transaction or think there may have been a misunderstanding between creditor and debtor, it will show when you talk to the debtor. Your position will be weakened. Instead of being able to say, "Mr. Debtor, I understand that you believe that there is a problem, however you have had a number of opportunities to resolve it," you would be more likely to weaken your position by saying something like,"Well gee, Mr. Jones, I'm sorry about your problem and perhaps I should look into it for you."

DEVELOP VERBAL AND MENTAL SKILLS

The collector who treats every debtor in the same way is severely limited. In talking with people you need to be versatile enough to deal with a professional person in one call and a blue collar worker in the next, without making either of them feel he is being talked up to or down to.

You have to stay mentally alert in order to cope with the perpetual stream of excuses and schemes you will hear. You must be ready to anticipate and overcome each of them, and you must be able to respond to whatever defenses or objections are given. This will take quick thinking, good imagination, and versatility. Do not allow yourself to lose your temper or you will lose the ability to be objective or quick-thinking.

Different people respond to different kinds of motivation. You will have to be alert to clues that provide you with three or four motivations to try, as you sell the debtor on the benefits that will be gained by paying the bill at once and in full. But you have to be creative and respond quickly. You can't sit there on the telephone and say, "Yes, Mr. Jones, nnnnn," while you decide what motivation to use. You have to immediately categorize why he didn't pay the bill and what you think he'll do now. What is he: A staller? A complainer? Will he pay right away? Will he commit to terms? You have to be ready to respond immediately. Because he is not going to wait.

CREATE WORD PICTURES

When an author describes a scene in his book, he's creating a word picture. You need to do the same, except that you are going to do it verbally. When you talk with debtors, you want them to visualize the problem you are discussing. It's up to you how graphic you want to be.

You probably wouldn't say, "Well, Mr. Sims, you know when your wife goes down the street to the store, you don't really want anybody saying, "There goes Mrs. Sims, the deadbeat's wife.' "

You probably wouldn't say, "Well, Mrs. Lee, you don't want to be lying out there in the middle of the road with all the blood coming down off your head and your arm on the right side of the street, and we're not going to take care of you."

You can make word pictures based on the motivation you are

using—to help the debtor to visualize the positive or negative result you're describing. You are making it easier for the debtor (to agree to pay) by spelling out the consequences if he does not pay.

One type of image is created when you describe the problem the debtor will have by not paying the bill:

"Mr. Williams, you really don't want me calling you every day, do you? You don't want to have me on your back and all of the other people who are involved in collecting this debt. Why don't we make an agreement of some sort."

You haven't created a big word picture there, but you have given him the idea of having to answer the phone every day. He doesn't want that, and he's going to make some kind of an agreement if he has any intention or ability to pay the bill.

If you think his credit rating is important to him, make him "see" what will happen if he loses it. If you have a clue that he is proud of his image in the community make sure he gets the picture of how he'll look to everyone after your legal action to collect gets into the papers. Assume that he wants to pay and that avoidance of embarrassment is a reason that will convince him that he wants to pay.

KNOW YOUR BUSINESS

It is human nature for debtors to have built up a good defense in their mind to rationalize why they have not paid a debt. You will be confronted regularly with a myriad of excuses. Knowing all you can about your company's policies, practices, products and/or services will help you recognize many imaginary grievances and stalls.

Let's say you call Mr. Fixit about his overdue bill, and he tells you that he is not going to pay it because the lawn mower he purchased didn't work properly. At this point the burden is on you to explain that the policy of the company is to replace any purchase that is defective. You ask him why he didn't return the lawn mower, since the problem would have been taken care of immediately. This shifts the responsibility back to him. If he is not able to give you a legitimate reason, then obviously you are dealing with a staller.

KNOW YOUR ACCOUNT

One way you can maintain control of your telephone interviews is to know so much about the debtor that you can counter his stalls or objections to paying the bill *("Mrs. Stanley, I know your company has a credit union; and since you have been employed there for five years, you more than qualify for a loan.")* and be ready to solve his financial dilemma *("The Hometown Tool Company gives bonuses about this time every year, and I hope you'll be able to use part of yours to clear up this account.")*.

That is why it is important to keep files, with a filled-out form for each customer. Many debtors are repeats and a check of your files can provide a head start. A little background as to family and marital status, where employed, and spouse's name will enable you to handle the conversation more knowledgeably.

DEVELOP TELEPHONE SKILLS

SPEAK CLEARLY

In face-to-face conversation, the listener can watch your lips and expressions. Since this is impossible in telephone conversations, be sure your diction is not sloppy. Speak clearly and distinctly and at a moderate speed. Use words and phrases that cannot possibly be misunderstood. Give the debtor a chance to assimilate what you say. The tone of your voice, pacing of words, emphasis and choice of words are important in creating impressions. Careless speech habits can confuse and frustrate your listener. Communications actually can break down, making your collection effort just that much more difficult.

BE TACTFUL

Make an effort to maintain the dignity of the person from whom you are collecting. At the same time you should try to talk to people on the level that they are used to understanding. Never offend debtors by correcting their speech. If they mispronounce a word and you have occasion to use the same word, try to find another one with the same meaning so you don't step on their ego by indirectly correcting them.

BE BUSINESSLIKE

Don't ever threaten the debtor. Don't ever shout at the debtor. Don't antagonize the debtor. Don't accuse him of being dishonest. Don't come across on the phone with a belligerent attitude, because it goes right through the phone to them and they'll come right back at you the same way. Did you ever start screaming at somebody on the phone and the other end screams back? It's the same thing in debt collection, except it gets worse. They have a reason to not like you.

Always address the individual as Mr. Brown or Mrs. Brown. This not only defines the formality and seriousness of the matter, but discourages the debtor from assuming an intimacy toward you. Addressing him by title also emphasizes the fact that you are treating him like a responsible adult, and therefore you can expect him to behave like one. So, even if he tells you to call him John, don't.

Another reason to be businesslike is that debtors are more likely to keep their promises if you keep them at arm's length. It's a business call and should be handled as a business call. Be courteous and firm. If you indicate any weakening on your part, they will begin to take control of the conversation.

BE A GOOD LISTENER

Many collectors fail to establish satisfactory communication with debtors because they do not listen to them. They may feel that whatever the debtor has to say is unimportant or will not be of any value in collecting the account. Or they start preaching to the debtor, thinking they are motivating by anxiety.

Inexperienced collectors have a tendency to overtalk the debtor. They have something they have planned to say, and they are thinking of that as the debtor is speaking; thus no communication takes place. And sometimes that can get embarrassing.

I'll never forget a conversation between a collector and a debtor that went something like this:

> *Debtor:* "I understand what you're saying and I'm not really sure that I can handle the entire account, but I can probably pay it off in the next 60 days."

> *Collector:* "Listen, if you're not going to offer me a payment schedule then I'm going to have to refer you to suit."

Be aware that in order to generate the necessary thought patterns in a debtor's mind, you must use words he understands and answer the questions that arise. Don't transmit a message for your own benefit, but rather for the benefit of the debtor. Your ultimate goal in communication is to make sure that both you and the debtor are thinking on the same wavelength.

3. BE INFORMED

DEBT COLLECTION IS, in a word, communication. The more convincingly that you can tell debtors what you want them to do (when and how to pay the bill), the more likely they will do it. And believe me, people want to be told what to do, especially the ones who have financial problems. They have so many debts they don't know which way to turn. They need help most of the time. Some of them recognize it; most of them don't.

Each time you make a call you must control the interview and lead the debtor to tell you why he hasn't paid, as well as how and when he is going to pay. You may have to motivate him to pay, and convince him to take action at the earliest possible moment. To be able to hold the advantage in the conversation, you need to know your debtor and you need to have the call organized ahead.

If you do not feel in control of the situation, even before you pick up the telephone, the debtor will sense your lack of confidence through your voice or your presentation, and you won't be as successful, if you succeed at all.

Before beginning to work on an account, scan it quickly to gain a preliminary insight into what you may be confronted with when debtor contact is made. Do you have all the information you need or will you have to get part of it from the debtor? By being prepared ahead of time, you can respond quickly, and your call will be much more effective.

59

The following information will be a big help in anticipating the objections you may get.

1. How much is owed?

2. What is the debt for? Specifically what goods or services were rendered.

3. Date of the last charge.

4. Date of the last payment.

5. Who made the last payment—a third party or the debtor?

6. How many attempts to contact debtor have been made? How many of these were by letter and how many by phone?

7. Present or last known address (and any other addresses known). Type of neighborhood? Buying or renting?

8. Occupation or employment of debtor (and of spouse). What type of work does he/she do? How long on job?

You need to know, too, if the account has been handled by any other collector. You don't want to be put in a position where the debtor says, "Hey, I just got a phone call yesterday from somebody else." You need to know what's going on, because it is embarrassing to find out from the debtor that someone else in your office has just been on that same case. It also annoys people and gets them to a point where they don't want to pay.

60

4. FINDING MISSING DEBTORS:
SKIPTRACING

SKIPTRACING IS THE PROCESS of collecting information about "skips" for the purpose of collecting outstanding debts. A "skip" is a debtor who has moved and who cannot be readily located by mail or by phone.

For accounts that are large enough to warrant the time and expense, you may prefer to try to find the debtor yourself rather than turn the account over to an agency. How and where you look for this information not only will determine how successful you will be, but it also could mean the difference between having a contented debtor who is cooperative once found and contacted, or a discontented one who might sue your office for invasion of privacy.

Fortunately, people are usually not successful at avoiding good collectors. They'll avoid the average collector easily — they'll move and they'll be very hard to find. But a good collector can almost always find them.

Before jumping to conclusions about a missing debtor, check your files. You may have recorded a new address and then neglected to transfer it to the correct file. You should also check the files of customers with similar names, especially those with the same last name. You may turn up a misfiled spouse, or a relative who can tell you where to find your debtor.

Sometimes you will find a person who has records in more than one file. You might find the name George B. Jones, for example, recorded in different ways, either through a clerical error or by intention of the debtor. As a result, Mr. Jones might owe money under the account names of George J. Jones, George Jones, Geo. B. Jones, G. B. Jones, George Burton Jones, and so on.

We have discovered such "lost" people in a number of collection cases, especially with utility, cable, and telephone companies, where checking for bad debts is likely to be done by computer. Even though these companies run a check for bad debt when someone first comes in for service—to have the telephone turned on, for example—the person who skips out on his debts knows that the computer checks for exact name match. Therefore, he can avoid being picked up by the computer by changing the middle initial or even by changing the spelling of a given name. He is thus able to avoid payment of the previous debt and get service again.

IS SKIPTRACING WORTH THE TIME AND EFFORT?

You will have to use your own judgment in deciding to what extent you should skiptrace. Every debtor could probably be located with the expenditure of enough time and money. However, the expense may exceed the benefits of collecting from difficult skips. Or you may know from past experience that you are not likely to be paid even after finding the person. Sometimes it is better to use an outside collection agency rather than spend too much time locating a skip.

Most skips fall into the category of *the unintentional skip*. They are individuals who tend to be careless about their obligations, so they make no attempt to keep in touch. However, they are not trying to keep their identity or address a secret, and once they are located, collection is generally easy.

62

The intentional skip is the individual who tries to prevent creditors from locating him/her. These will be more difficult to find and, once found, may not pay.

There are also *skips resulting from marital difficulties.* In these cases, the individual would rather the spouse pay the bills, but really doesn't care if the bills are paid or not. Here, the amount owed may help you decide whether to pursue the collection or turn the account over to a collection agency.

HOW TO BEGIN

If you have photocopied the driver's license, it will give you a starting point when you can't locate someone. Many of the state driver's license divisions will give you all the information they have, such as last address, physical description, and insurance carrier. For some reason, people notify the drivers license division of their new address when they move. (Another benefit of photocopying the driver's license is that you can have the face to go with the voice on the phone. It is a psychological advantage to know what your contact looks like.)

It used to be possible to trace people from their social security numbers. We could send in a social security number to the government and they would tell us where the person was working, or give us the last employer. Then the federal government, in its infinite wisdom, took the position that social security information was no longer to be given out to the general public.

The following are good "tools" to have on hand as you search for skips:

1. Telephone directory for your own and nearby cities. Don't overlook the telephone company's new listings. Your skip may have had a new phone connected in his own name.

2.   Directory of post offices.

3.   City map and city directory. These can help if you have the name of the spouse or the name of a neighbor.

4.   Chamber of commerce membership roster.

5.   Military base directories.

6.   Student directories (high schools, colleges, etc.)

The following is the information you will want to develop on each skip in order to locate him:

1.   Debtor's correct and full name, spelled correctly. Is he a Junior or Senior?

2.   Social security number.

3.   Complete and correct address, including street number and name, and zip code. If the address is out of town, get the city and state. If you are in an area where there are similar names in a city and in adjoining towns, make sure you have the right name and the correct spelling.

4.   Former address. Check for former landlord, as this may provide many good leads.

5.   Place of employment as well as occupation or type of work or trade. Many people can be traced relatively easily through their type of work. A car salesman will tend to remain a car salesman, even after he skips. Therefore, look for job-related organizations or trade unions listed in the yellow pages, once you know the city where the debtor has moved.

6.   Employment address for both husband and wife; in the case of single people living with parents, the employment addresses of the parents. Get information as to position, length of employment, earnings, and payday. If

you only have a former employer to talk to, check for references. Ask for inquiries that have been made since the debtor left the employment and ask where the W-2 tax form was sent.

7. Real estate. Does the debtor rent, lease, or own property? If the debtor owns, you may be able to find the name of the mortgagor. Or the insurance broker who handled the insurance on the house. If the debtor rents, you want to have the landlord's name and address. For apartments, the name of the superintendent or rental office manager.

8. Personal property. Develop information as to the ownership of a car and the name of the financing company holding the title. Find out if the debtor has a checking or savings account and the possibility of the debtor having a credit union loan or having had one at a former place of employment. Many times a debtor will have an accident case pending and although it has not been settled, it may provide a possibility of collection.

9. Names of relatives and friends. These are reliable sources of information, and although not all relatives will cooperate, at least you find a large percentage who will if they are approached properly. Friends of the debtor may provide valuable leads.

   If you ask new customers to fill out personal information on a form (as part of office policy), the name, address, and phone number of a relative who does not live with them can be invaluable. This person may know how to locate their missing relative.

The following are all sources that can be checked for information about skips:

1. Your files. Review all pending, filed, or paid orders.

2. Neighbors and friends. They may know about the debtor's church, bowling team, favorite tavern, hobbies, lodge,

65

union affiliation, clubs, social habits, etc.

3. Neighborhood stores. Service stations, barbers, beauty shops, etc., may have valuable leads.

4. Older children and elderly people. They frequently can be helpful. Guide them and let them talk.

5. Former employers. Talk to the owner, manager, or personnel department (depending on the size of the business). Frequently the bookkeeper can tell you where the debtor's W-2 form was sent.

6. Fellow employees and friends. Try to obtain names of any special friends, get addresses, and follow up.

7. Landlords, janitors, superintendents of apartments. These people can frequently give leads such as the name of the moving company, good friends of the skip, etc.

8. Neighbors. They can be an excellent source of data on the skip. What moving company van moved the furniture? What are the names of the debtor's friends or relatives? Any leads might provide information as to location of the skip, even though the neighbors may not know where he/she is.

9. Local newspapers. Data relating to your debtor may be in the master files. You should get into the habit of reading the "vital statistics" — suits filed, property bought and sold, etc. — every day. You will be amazed at how often you recognize the name of someone you have been trying to collect from or to locate.

10. Finance companies. They have excellent "skip sheets" on every loan made. Establish good relations with all area finance companies.

11. Labor unions. Contact local labor union office for current address or current employer.

12. People with same or similar names in the phone book. Call them. They may know the skip and they may even be related.

13. Government records (federal, state, city, and town): real estate records, mortgages, deeds; personal property records; divorce and probate records; water department records; dog and fishing license records; marriage records; motor vehicle records; criminal and civil records; post office department. For a small fee you may send the post office any name with the last known address and they will search their records and give you the new address or the information they have. (Send to Postmaster, Mailing Requirements, your city and state.)

    Do not overlook any records that are considered public. Records that are maintained by government agencies or records of government employees are open for access. In many states, employment records of government employees are public. You might also check any of the following: registration of mortgages and liens; registration of trades (such as auto mechanics, insurance salespeople, taxi drivers, security guards); licensing boards for many types of professionals; arrest records. Obviously the debt size has to be large enough to warrant the amount of time that this kind of investigation takes.

14. Utility companies. Establish a good relationship with gas and electric company officials, but don't abuse it. Some utility companies publish a monthly change sheet of all their customers. If this is available, it can be invaluable. It only takes one phone call to find out if the person you can't find is on the utility register. It's amazing what you can turn up.

    The Deadbeat family seemed to have not paying bills down to a science. They owed the hospital (our client)

67

over $35,000 and had avoided us for three and a half years.

They also did not pay their electric bill. Every three months when the cut-off notice came, a different member of the family would open a new account and pay a new deposit, and the power would go on in that person's name. There were eighteen people in the family. They had a mama, a papa, a grandpa and a grandma, and fourteen kids. They never used the same last name, so there was no continuity to their records. The power went on for Patricia Sally, for example. Or Billy Joe. Patricia Sally might have been three months old.

You cannot imagine the amount of work that went into finding these people. The way we finally found them was with an address check through the utility records. We discovered all these different accounts for the same address.

SEQUENCE OF THE SKIPTRACE CALL

1. Identify the informant: *"Is this Mrs. James Colby at 3252 North Elmwood Street?"*

2. Identify yourself: *"Mrs. Colby, this is Andrew Stevens."*

3. State the problem: *"I need to get in touch with John Deadbeat."*

4. Ask for help: *"Can you help me?"*

5. Listen — the psychological pause. Listen for attitude; listen for leads; listen for a lead to another informant.

6. Ask yourself if the informant knows where the skip is.

7. Ask the informant: *"Do you know where he is? Do you know who else can help me?"*

8. Be prepared for the informant to ask two key questions: *"Who did you say this was?"* and *"What do you want him for?"* (The way you answer his questions will determine whether he works with you or against you. Try to combine your answers with a question of your own.)

9. Thank the informant.

When you announce who you are immediately, in some cases you will not be asked what company you represent. Remember that in your contacts with relatives, friends, or other parties you should not give information as to why you are calling, in order to avoid embarrassment to the debtor.

When you are attempting to locate a debtor and you are talking to anyone but the spouse or the debtor, you have to avoid putting yourself in the illegal position of revealing the nature of your call. Federal guidelines specify that debt collectors may not reveal the nature of their call (if it has to do with a collection effort) to anyone outside the immediate family of the debtor.

Therefore, it is especially important that you do not tell the informant the reason for your call. If someone asks, simply say that your call is a personal business call or that it has to do with a business matter.

ESSENTIAL CHARACTERISTICS
OF A GOOD SKIPTRACER

A GOOD TELEPHONE VOICE

You should have a well-modulated and friendly voice that asks for assistance and information and does not demand it. You should be friendly by nature as well as businesslike in your approach. If you are friendly and warm, you will get people to give information that otherwise could not be obtained.

PATIENCE

Whenever you call an informant, you never know what situation you will find at the other end of the line. For example, the person who answers may be on the way out or late for work. If you are patient, you will be able to set up a time to call back or may even hold the informant long enough to complete the call.

TACT

You must have the technique of being able to bring out information by asking tactful leading questions.

The sensitivity with which you gather the necessary information about the debtor can affect the attitude of the debtor at the time of contact and can be a definite asset to you in attempting to get PIF (Payment In Full).

POSITIVE BENEFITS OF PAYING

Good credit return.
The satisfaction of fulfilling an obligation.
Reputation for fair play.
Self-respect.
Freedom from worry.
Security on the job.
Security for the family.
Good example for the children.
Opportunity to return for further credit.

PART III

THE COLLECTION CALL

COLLECTION CALL SEQUENCE

Preparation
1. Plan your call.
2. Have all tools ready.
3. Be prepared to take control.

The Opening of the Call
1. Be positive.
2. Identify the person with whom you are speaking.
3. Identify yourself.
4. State the reason for your call.

The Body of the Call
1. Ask for Payment In Full.
2. Disregard the initial objection.
3. Be positive.
4. Control the conversation but do not overtalk the debtor.
5. Ask questions.
6. Get information.
7. Watch for closing clues.
8. Use trial closes.
9. Sell benefits and control environment.
10. Don't argue.
11. Overcome objections.
12. Resell benefits.
13. Reassure debtor that he/she is making the right decision.
14. Offer debtor alternative solutions.
15. Close!

How to Close a Call
1. Make it easy for the debtor to say yes.
2. Have debtor write your address down and repeat it to you.
3. Review terms and dramatize importance of keeping arrangement.

1. THE OPENING

Be positive.
Identify the person with whom you are speaking.
Identify yourself.
State the reason for your call.

THE MESSAGE YOU WANT to convey to the debtor is simple. So, be brief. You achieve your maximum effect during the first few seconds on the phone.

Remember to address your debtor frequently by name and state your case with conviction and assurance. Make sure the person is listening and that you have his or her attention. Be courteous, firm, and businesslike. Take the initiative and be persistent. Never allow your feelings to get the better of you. Anger and indignation actually defeat your collection efforts.

IDENTIFY THE PERSON WITH WHOM YOU ARE SPEAKING AND VERIFY INFORMATION

The first thing that you do in making the call is to make sure you are taking to the right person. You should not assume the person who answers the phone is the one you are calling. Be specific in establishing his/her identity.

73

"Hello, is this James M. David of 320 East Main Street?"

If you are not talking to the debtor, then be sure you are talking to the spouse or other person responsible for paying the account. (Your records should indicate the responsible parties.) Verify the spelling of the name, the address, and the place of employment.

"Do you still work at . . . ?"

By confirming the address, you may learn that the debtor has moved to a new location, even though the telephone number hasn't changed.

If the person you need to reach is not there, you may leave your name but do not give anyone the reason for your call. Indebtedness, legally, has become a sensitive issue, and embarrassing the debtor could give him grounds for lawsuit. If asked for a message, simply say it is a personal or business matter.

IDENTIFY YOURSELF AND GIVE
THE REASON FOR YOUR CALL

Once you know that you are talking to the right party, identify yourself, who you represent, and the reason you are calling.

"Mr. Jones, my name is Leonard Bendell and I represent the County Regional Medical Center, and I am calling today in reference to the account that you owe, which is $684, and which, as you are aware, is overdue by about ninety days."

2. THE BODY OF THE CALL

Be positive.
Ask for Payment In Full.
Disregard the initial objection.
Control the conversation but do not overtalk the debtor.
Ask questions.
Get information.
Watch for closing clues.
Use trial closes.
Sell benefits of paying.
Don't argue, preach, judge, or moralize.
Overcome objections.
Offer solutions.
Resell benefits of paying.
Reassure debtor that he is making the right decision.

REREAD THE ITEMS on this list before every call until they become second nature to you. Try to remember them in every phone call to debtors.

ASK FOR PAYMENT IN FULL

What do you want the debtor to do? Pay in full. You are always going to ask for Payment In Full. Make your statement courteous but firm:

"As you know, your account with the Delkor Department Store is seriously overdue. Will you bring your check for $65 to our office by 5 o'clock this afternoon, please?"

When you talk to debtors on the telephone, you must convey a sense of urgency, making them feel they must take care of the debt now! If you don't, they know they can put you off. You can create urgency by setting deadlines.

"I've just been handed this account and I have to make a report on it tomorrow."

"I need your payment no later than Friday."

Never offer a payment agreement. You may accept one, but do not offer one. Insist upon Payment In Full, convince the debtor that the matter is urgent, and keep calm and cheerful at all times.

Always assume they are always going to pay. Never make a phone call without that assumption. "Hi, Mrs. Jones, you are going to pay today, right?" If you have the attitude that Mrs. Jones will pay, if everything you do is positive and you believe there is no way she is not going to pay, most of the time she'll pay; she'll make an agreement, and she'll keep that agreement.

The banking industry uses the philosophy, "three days and never later than Friday." The typical bank collector is instructed to never accept an offer of payment that extends beyond three days or the following Friday, whichever comes first. They are very serious about it. If I owe the bank $300 on an installment payment and I can't pay now but know I can pay in two weeks, most bank collectors are not authorized to accept my payment in two weeks. I can tell you it generally works.

THE PSYCHOLOGICAL PAUSE

What is the next thing you do? Nothing! Don't say another word! If it takes seven minutes, don't say another word. We call this the psychological pause because it puts the burden of conversation on the debtor. He has to respond. He may sit there and play a waiting game. Normally, though, after about twenty seconds of dead silence, he will respond. *He will almost always, in the very first few words, give you the reasons for the delinquency.*

"I want to pay, but I just don't have the money."

"I know it was my child in the hospital, but her father is responsible for the bill."

"The insurance is supposed to cover it, so you have to get the money from the insurance company."

"My wife (or husband) pays the bills."

"The medicine (or the TV) didn't work."

BE A GOOD LISTENER

You must listen to what the debtor has to say. Listening is difficult. It can be especially painful when you have a comment to make and are waiting for your party to finish. The only way you will gain information is by keeping your ears open and your mouth closed. There may be a reason for non-payment that will require a different approach on your part.

Debtors don't recognize it most of the time, but they will almost inevitably tell you how they can pay. By careful listening you can pick up the clues that will lead to sources of money for them. Any time you can solve the problem, or can help the debtor solve the problem, you may get the money faster.

You may be able to use the information you get to close the conversation right there. If she tells you why she hasn't paid, but that she is going to pay, say, "Fine, when may we expect payment?" Close the sale.

On the other hand, the debtor's first words may be a barrage of profanity as he lashes out in anger. Don't let him rattle you. Instead, try to understand him as an individual and try to see the situation from his side. You may be the fourth person who has called for payment in the past hour. The last caller may have threatened to repossess his car or take him to court. Or, he may be angry because he has a legitimate, valid reason for not paying, and he assumes you won't listen. Just remember to treat all the people on the other end of the phone as you would like to be treated in that same situation, and be patient until you learn the reason the debtor hasn't paid the bill.

You can't let hostile, angry individuals make you react in a hostile and angry manner, or you won't collect a cent. You have to remember that they're not mad at you, they're mad at themselves. All they are doing is getting their frustration out. Once they do that, you can talk to them. So, stay calm and pleasant, and they will eventually calm down.

Sometimes a hostile debtor will hang up the phone on you. You can handle it by dialing right back and saying, "Are you finished?" or "Can we talk now?" You may be burning inside, but you have to speak calmly, with no anger. It takes the debtor totally off guard!

CATEGORIZE BY ANTICIPATED RESULTS

As soon as a debtor gives you the reason why he/she has not paid, you will have an opinion as to how the account will be resolved. Even though you may gain new information during the conversation or afterwards, that changes your opinion, you need to identify your thoughts as to whether and/or how you will be paid. These are the categories:

INDIVIDUALS WHO PAY ON FIRST DEMAND

These people are a collector's delight. They bring in or send the money and all you have to do is write a receipt and close the file.

If the debtor tells you he has overlooked the bill but now that you've called it to his attention he will send a check, or he has been short of funds but can pay now, you can end the call right there. Or you may know from previous contact with this person (or the files) that he is more likely stalling. How you categorize him will determine the direction of your conversation.

INDIVIDUALS WHO CAN'T PAY IN FULL,
BUT WILL MAKE ARRANGEMENTS TO DO SO

Usually included in this classification are the big spenders (spendthrifts who have never learned self-denial), poor budgeters (frequently easygoing and sometimes not-too-intelligent persons who buy almost anything that anyone will sell them on credit), victims of adverse circumstances (people who normally pay their bills promptly), armed forces personnel (who can usually be persuaded to honor their obligations), and those with limited income or large families (their circumstances make payment difficult, but you can usually find a solution).

You've got to exhaust all efforts of obtaining Payment In Full. Many times, by checking the file and talking with him, you will determine that a debtor who agrees to make arrangements to pay is actually able to pay the account in full immediately.

When a debtor has stated that he cannot pay in full, and you learn the reason and your suggestions for money sources prove negative, you must not ask him, "How much can you pay?" That places him in control. Should he make an offer you can't accept, you will find it very difficult to increase that offer. You might ask him how much he is short of the amount he owes. Or remind him that credit reputation is measured by the length of time it takes to pay a debt. The longer it takes, the more reluctant creditors become in providing credit the next time it is needed.

But don't consent to small weekly payments either. Always refuse the first figure he suggests; he can almost always do better. On the other hand, there isn't any sense in getting a person to agree to pay $200 per month on a bad debt when you know that he can't afford $200 a month. Is he going to maintain his payment schedule? Of course he isn't. So all the work you have done is for nothing. If you are going to collect the money, if you are going to get the debtor on a schedule to pay, make it a schedule that he can live with.

Look at the debtor's economic situation realistically before you decide to accept an arrangement for term payments. If someone has had an account with you for some time, the size of the average balance compared to what it was a few years ago may be a clue to payment terms. Be careful to use a realistic time frame—short enough for the arrangements to be profitable, but long enough so that the debtor can meet the payments.

Have you ever handled an account that had been set up by someone else, and when you called on a broken promise the debtor said, "I just couldn't pay $40 every week but the girl insisted that this was the only amount she would accept."

The facts established that this person could not pay more than $20 a week, yet the first collector merely pushed and pressured and used anxiety motivation with little regard for the information that indicated that $40 a week would be impossible.

You obviously are not concerned with somebody else's bill that that same person might owe. But you have to remember that he has to handle that collector as well. If you take all the money, you are right back to the guy who screams loudest and first gets paid, which means next month you have to start over.

INDIVIDUALS WHO HAVE A GRIEVANCE OR DISPUTE

Because many debtors offer an excuse for not paying, and since most complaints get settled before they reach the collector, you must learn to discriminate between a legitimate grievance (the bill will most likely be paid if the grievance is satisfactorily resolved) and a stall.

It is incumbent upon you to remove all doubt regarding the complaint. The debtor may have complained a number of times to other people who haven't done anything about it. If you believe there is the slightest chance the complaint is valid, take the information, say "Thank you very much; we'll get back to you." Then check it out. You don't want to put yourself into the position of not promoting good will. If the complaint is not valid, call back and say, "Your complaint is not valid. We have found out the following facts." If the dispute is not valid, then it is a stall.

STALLERS

With experience, you will learn to recognize stallers. They are the ones who give every reason imaginable to delay paying the account. They demand itemized billings, or they owe you $1,000 and send you $5 a week. They tell you the three big lies that collectors hear: "The check is in the mail." "I didn't get your bill." "Give me another week and I'll take care of it." They create imaginary disputes (which you'll have to distinguish from legitimate complaints): "It didn't work," "It was damaged when I got it," "The doctor didn't cure my cold," "My appendix is still half in."

If the person has owed you money before, or has already shown stalling tactics on this bill, the records should give you enough clues to know that the excuses and promises are not valid.

In dealing with this type of debtor, who may be juggling many debts, it becomes necessary to create a sense of urgency regarding payment of the account.

Finding out from debtors which group they belong to is an ongoing classification process. Throughout your conversation, as their category changes, so will your approach change to fit the new circumstances. For example:

Debtor: I have no intention of paying this bill. When I got home I found that one part of the coffeemaker was broken. *(Apparent grievance.)*

Collector: Our policy is clearly stated on your invoice as well as in the store. We will fix or replace, at your option, any purchase that is not in perfect working order. Why didn't you bring it back three months ago?

Debtor: Well, I did finally get the thing assembled and working . . . . *(Now you know he's really a staller.)*

Collector: Then I need payment immediately. Will you be able to bring in a check for $39 before we close today at 5?

Debtor: I'll mail you $5 on the account today. I can't pay any more than that right now. *(Another stall.)*

Collector: This account is over 90 days overdue and I have to settle it today. How much are you short of the $39?

Debtor: Maybe I could send you $10 a week. *(Clue that he will agree to terms.)*

Collector: I can't accept that. Our policy is to send accounts this old to our collection agency, and it would show up on your credit records then. If you could put the entire amount on your VISA or MasterCard, you would have a month before you would have to pay, and I wouldn't have to bother you again.

Debtor: Oh, all right. My card number is_____.

DEBTORS WHO REFUSE TO PAY BUT *CAN* BE MOTIVATED TO PAY

Usually these individuals begin by being very emphatic about not paying. They may embellish their refusal with some choice bits of profanity. They may slam the phone down. (It is interesting that more women hang up on you than men.)

Some people who refuse to pay are bluffing. They may believe that you will not (or cannot) take steps to force payment. Some see the process as a game. We have had people come in, sit down, and actually joke about how we beat them. They've been trying to beat us and boy, they just couldn't get past us! We've had others come in and gleefully tell how they beat us.

Most of those who refuse to pay can be convinced that paying will be better for them than not paying (see "Motivating the Debtor," page 93). These debtors will require your best sales efforts and your most energy and creativity.

If your best sales efforts fail to convince them, you will have to resort to third party referral, for a search for assets and involuntary collection methods. (The procedure belongs in your Collections Policy.)

DEBORS WHO REFUSE TO PAY AND *CANNOT* BE MOTIVATED TO PAY

This category consists of two groups: hardship cases (those who will never have the money to pay the bill), who are sometimes handicapped as well, and frauds (credit criminals).

True hardship cases are usually honest persons who intended to pay. However, they are simply unable to earn enough, and there is nothing you can do that will ever enable them to come up with the money. These accounts should be closed immediately upon recognition, as the time you will expend will not justify the return.

There is also no point in wasting your time pursuing deadbeats who never intended to pay in the first place. These debtors will "beat" you every time because they are serious about it. You may never be able to reach them by phone, but if you do they are likely to tell you just where to go and then hang up on you.

These are credit criminal who have no regard for their credit reputation. They put their assets in somebody else's name, they move frequently, they often use variations on their given name —anything to throw creditors off the track. Fortunately, they consititute only about three percent of the debtor population. Realize that you will never collect a dime, and nobody else will either. Most creditors will write these accounts off, realizing they should not have extended credit in the first place.

About skips. Even though many credit criminals become skips, not all skips are intentionally evading their creditors. There is a difference. An apparent skip may be someone who has moved and, in the haste of leaving, has forgotten to give a forwarding address. Perhaps he/she relied on someone else to do it. Sometimes a skip begins in this innocent manner, but as time goes by and nothing happens, the person becomes less inclined to consider the debt as an obligation. In dealing with a skip, consider the action as an innocent oversight until you have reason to believe otherwise.

A DUNNER IS NOT A COLLECTOR

The telephone "dunner" concentrates on volume production, relating a fast message of demand to debtors contacted. The dunner gets on the phone with a piece of paper or a computer terminal in front of him and says, "Mrs. Jones, I am so-and-so and you owe us $150. When can we expect your money?" Mrs. Jones starts to spill out all the reasons why she can't pay, but the dunner doesn't listen. He just says, "We expect your money by 5 o'clock tomorrow. Thank you very much, good bye." Little, if any consideration is given to her ability to meet this demand.

Is Mrs. Jones going to be paying her bill? No. She isn't going to pay because the dunner didn't attempt to overcome any of her reasons for not paying. Mrs. Jones has a lot of reasons why she hasn't paid it in the past, and she has reasons why she may not be able to pay it in the near future.

Dunners don't pay any attention to what the debtor is telling them. Many times they respond to the debtor's antagonism by being antagonistic. If a debtor screams in defense, a dunner is likely to scream right back. Dunners sometimes threaten without ever having the intent to follow through on their threats.

The professional collector treats debtors as individuals. He or she listens to their reasons for not paying and works with them to find solutions to their problems. The collector finds ways to motivate them to pay, by giving them more reasons to pay the bill than they have for not paying it.

By listening, helping, and motivating, the collector is frequently able to obtain payment and maintain her good will at the same time. Collecting has to be approached from a psychological point of view, or you will never collect any money. A dunner may receive small sums from time to time, but he will never "collect," and he will never maintain the debtor's good will.

Being a collector involves understanding the type of individual you are dealing with and why he or she has not paid the bill, listening to the reason given for not paying in order to anticipate results and find motivations he or she will respond to, and applying that motivation to overcoming the debtor's objections to paying that bill.

TELEPHONE DO'S AND DON'TS

DO: Know all the details about your account.

Have confidence in your claim.

Identify the person answering your call.

Keep calm and cheerful.

Insist on Payment In Full.

Treat all debtors as you would want to be treated.

Remember the consumer may be right. (Get the details if the account is disputed.)

Be businesslike, courteous, and natural.

Keep the conversation alive. If there is a coolness at the beginning of the conversation, introduce some point of mutual agreement.

Exhibit an interest in the person. Listen to his or her story.

Find out if the debtor considers the obligation important. Discuss the debtor's attitudes and why the debtor takes the position he/she does.

Determine how much interest the debtor has in finding a solution to his/her difficulties. Inquire regarding the steps already taken to resolve these problems.

Take notes during the call.

Let person know you want to be fair.

DON'T: Threaten the debtor, ever.

Shout at the debtor.

Antagonize the debtor.

Argue, preach, judge, or moralize.

Consider all debtors as credit criminals.

Accuse the debtor of being dishonest.

Use a hard-boiled attitude.

Consent to small weekly payments until you're sure that all efforts have been exhausted for obtaining PIF.

Overlook any possibilities of obtaining PIF by suggesting money sources.

3. FINDING THE SOLUTION

When somebody picks up his car after it has been repaired, and doesn't pay, he is essentially saying "IOU." The letters I, O, and U mean "I owe you money and will pay it on whatever terms we agreed on." They also stand for Imagination, Originality, and Urgency, necessary traits for a good collector.

MANY DEBTORS GET BEYOND the point where they are able to handle their own problems. They actually need to be shown how they can pay. This is something that a lot of collectors don't really do. Your competitive edge — over every other place where they also owe money and every other place where they could spend it — is to offer help.

If the debtor does not promise immediate payment, you may be able to achieve Payment In Full simply by being aware that he/she will probably receive a Christmas bonus or an income tax refund. You may know that the employer gives quarterly bonuses. You might even suggest that the debtor ask for a raise.

Be creative and don't be afraid to attempt any new approach you can think of. You will be surprised at the results. Even though it is sometimes discouraging trying to work out these problems with debtors, compare that with the time spent calling continually to get them to resume weekly payments.

Maintain a courteous, considerate, and helpful relationship, but assume leadership in finding a solution to payment. As you offer solutions, remember to frame your questions so as to evoke a "yes" response. Without being offensive, take it for granted that the debtor will answer in the affirmative. You can say, "I know you want to get this cleared up. Will you mail a check or bring it in yourself?" If you know (from your records) that the person belongs to a credit union, you might say, "You can borrow the money from your credit union, can't you?" Lead the debtor to develop a definite plan of action that will clear the account in full. Withhold agreement to accept partial payment until all facts indicate that there is no other feasible alternative.

BUDGETING

Many people have never understood the value of budgeting. If you have gained the debtor's confidence, and are confident of your own abilities, you could help the debtor set up a budget and a payment schedule. There are also credit counseling services offered at no cost in almost every community. Most people have no idea that this kind of help is available.

LOANS

Perhaps a debtor is not be able to pay $40 a week, but may well be able to pay in full. How? By refinancing an existing loan or by obtaining a loan through a credit union or bank (which often offer the lowest interest rates), or finance company (which may make a loan to people who do not qualify for bank loans), or by selling something of value he owns.

Many people will not have considered consolidating their indebtedness into one loan, and that may be all they need in order to pay what they owe you. Similarly, selling the debtor on the idea of refinancing can be the key to Payment In Full, a satisfied client, and more profits for your office.

CREDIT CARD

If you are set up to accept credit card payments, you might suggest that the debtor charge the balance owed you on a credit card. You can achieve Payment In Full and at the same time it allows the debtor to postpone payment another thirty days.

POSTDATED CHECKS

Basically, postdated checks are nothing more than a written promise to pay, and they are very difficult prosecute if returned by the bank. Postdated checks present their own kind of problem. According to the Federal Fair Debt Collection Practices Act, you must notify the debtor in writing before depositing the check. You should also check your local laws.

Possibly a better option to consider would be to accept checks with the current date, and make an agreement with the debtor that you will hold them until an agreed-upon date or dates, at which time deposit would be made.

SELLING SOMETHING OF VALUE

When you talk to debtors, learn about their hobbies. These can sometimes provide clues to sources of cash. Frequently people have something of value without realizing it.

Several years ago, we had a hospital collection that was for about $45,000. The man really felt bad about the bill, and he had come to our office because he wanted to pay. But he was unemployed, indigent, with absolutely no ability to pay. Our conversation covered the usual topics—immediate ways to raise money, like loans and the credit union—and we also talked about his hobbies and diversions. Many times we find helpful ideas that way.

The man said to us, "Well, to tell you the truth, I've had a stamp collection for seventy years that my father gave me, and I've been adding to it." I asked him if there might be anything of value in the collection. He responded by bringing in about four stamp books a few days later.

We had a philatelist look at them, and the man walked out with a check for over $100,000! One of the stamps was very rare—one of four ever made, an inverted bi-plane—and alone worth $60,000! The man hadn't the faintest idea that he had this gold mine in his home. He paid the hospital in full, put money in his bank, and had security for the rest of his life.

A woman we collected from had a plate collection: a whole series of Royal Copenhagen Christmas plates. These beautiful plates are issued every year, and they increase in value every year. She would not sell the plates, which were worth almost $20,000, but we were able to get her to use them as collateral for a bank loan that paid off all her debts. She had had no idea that these plates were anything more than pretty dishes her mother had given her, that she'd been adding to over the years.

You can't ever think that because someone looks down and out that he/she can't pay until you've exhausted every effort to be sure. So, be alert as you talk to people, listen for clues as to how you can help them, find out what they have that may be of value. You have to be curious and imaginative.

CONTROLLING THE CONVERSATION

When you make a collection call, you will be following a sequence proven to lead debtors to pay. You can only follow this sequence by being in control of the conversation. Therefore you must not allow the debtor to lead the conversation away from your sequence. He may, for example, enjoy having someone to talk to, and want to describe the details of his accident, operation, or divorce. Your manner should be detached. You cannot get involved in debtors' problems, or you will lose control of the conversation. You can show empathy, however, and understand and counsel them with their problems. But always bring the conversation back to *your* topic: *"Will you be able to bring in a check...?"*

ABC'S OF TELEPHONE COLLECTING

ANTICIPATE your needs before you start your call; have all the information and tools on hand that you might need.

BELIEVE in your ability. If you have confidence in yourself, you are more easily able to accomplish what you set out to do.

CONTROL the conversation. Be firm and businesslike and keep in mind your goal of a Payment In Full (PIF).

DEVELOP a "third ear"; listen closely for clues to help you collect, both in what is said and in how it is said.

ENCOURAGE debtors to talk; let them tell their own stories in their own way.

FOCUS attention on developing a definite plan of action that will clear up the account in full.

GUARD against showing any signs of belligerence; a good collector can't afford a bad temper.

HELP the debtors find ways to meet their obligation; discuss possible sources of money with them.

IDENTIFY the debtor, yourself, the creditor and the amount of the claim; be sure you are talking to the debtor or his/her spouse, or the person who will pay the account.

JOT DOWN notes as you talk to the debtor; don't trust your memory——you need an accurate record of your telephone interview.

KEY your approach to what you know about the debtor; take into account the person's background and probable attitudes.

LEAD the debtor to develop a plan of action that will clear up the account in full.

MOTIVATE debtors to pay; the three basic appeals are honesty, pride, and fear or anxiety.

NEGOTIATE the most advantageous settlement possible if you are not able to obtain a Payment In Full.

OBSERVE any signs of the debtor's holding back information or making inconsistent statements; these may be a clue to his/her intentions.

PAUSE for a short time after opening the conversation; this throws the burden of conversation on the debtor and gives the debtor the chance to offer payment or to give the reason for not paying.

QUENCH any tendency you have to preach, moralize, judge, or argue; avoid fighting words.

REVIEW the debtor's work card; if there have been previous broken promises, you will want to keep a close check on any payment arrangements he/she may make.

SELL the debtor on the benefits to him/her of a PIF. SELECT a punch line to fit the debtor's situation. STRESS the urgency of the matter.

TALK clearly and distinctly when making a collection call; if you tend to speak fast, train yourself to slow down so there is no chance of the debtor's misunderstanding you.

UTILIZE your mistakes; they will help you do a better job if you let yourself learn from them.

VARY your approach; if you sense you're not getting through to a particular debtor, try a different approach.

WITHHOLD agreement to accept a partial payment until you are fully satisfied there is no other feasible means of collection.

X-RAY all the facts. If you find a problem you can't solve, refer the account to a more experienced collector in your office.

YIELD only when you are convinced that there is real hardship or the claim is impossible to collect.

ZERO IN on every call you make; persistence and patience pay off.

4. MOTIVATING THE DEBTOR

CMA x U = PIF. This is a collections industry acronym that stands for correct motivational appeal times you (your abilities) = Payment In Full.

EACH DEBTOR IS an individual with a different set of problems and each will react differently to your collection efforts. An approach that works for one person may not have any effect on another. It would seem, then, that no two people are alike and that you're on your own in an uncharted sea of human behavior.

Fortunately, that is not so. You are going to be able to draw upon what is known about people in general to fill out what you don't know about the debtor. For example, people in debt generally are in conflict. They feel impelled to pay the debt, but they do not want to.

People may spend every cent they make for new purchases, but they are not very willing to part with their money for a purchase or service that is no longer recent. Time has dulled its value, and they think of it as a current expense with no current benefit. *They will remit only if one of two things happens: their motivation for paying becomes stronger than their reason for not paying, or their resistances are weakened.*

Motivation may arise from guilt, anxiety or fear, or a desire to get more credit; resistence may be lowered with a tax refund, loan, or raise. With effective techniques, you will be able to find many ways to increase their motivation to pay or lessen their resistance.

Obviously, not everyone is motivated by the same emotional appeals. A salesperson who tries to sell you a new car knows this, so he appeals to your practicality: the car has a 5-year warranty; it gets 35 miles to the gallon. He might try to motivate another customer with an appeal to his ego: behind the wheel of this handsome car he'll feel like the success he's always wanted to be.

A classic example of how motivation affects collections is the "refrigerator case."

> If you owed me $100 for repairing a chair, you might insist that you don't have the money and you can't afford to pay me. But if your refrigerator broke and all the food was going bad, you would find a way to pay $100 to have it repaired.

It becomes a matter of need. Your success as a collector lies in motivating each person to satisfy some need. You have to show your debtors that their need to pay the bill for the repair of a chair or a visit to the dentist is just as important, in a different way, as repairing the refrigerator to save the food.

A collector encounters debtors in a special situation. They are anxious. They fear financial loss, loss of reputation, a lawsuit, they will not get credit in the future, or "something" will happen. Often, they feel guilty or ashamed and seek restoration of self-worth. They want others to think well of them so they can think well of themselves. They want to "square themselves" with the collector, the company, themselves. Such impulses are part of a person's needs.

It is human nature to want to satisfy five basic needs:

1. Physical
2. Security
3. Social
4. Ego
5. Self-fulfillment

In talking with debtors, you must discover their vulnerability: which needs, when appealed to, are most likely to motivate payment. The more basic the need, the more chance your appeal to that need has of motivating someone.

In using these needs as motivators, you will combine them with appeals to the debtor's *honesty and integrity*, or *pride*, or *fears and anxiety*.

Honesty. Honesty can satisfy social or ego needs: an honest person doesn't take something without paying for it; it's right to pay and wrong not to pay; the debtor is a trustworthy person; the debtor needs to square him/herself with the collector, company, and self; the debtor has a good payment record; the debtor is showing good faith (by paying). A reference to simple honesty may work especially well with an older person who was brought up when credit was not used as much as it is today.

Pride. Pride can satisfy social, ego, or self-fulfillment needs: the debtor keeps self-respect, sets a good example, is thought of as honest person; the debtor doesn't want to be denied credit; the debtor's image and what friends think about him/her is important; standing in the community is important; the debtor has a desire to do the right thing.

Anxiety. Anxiety can be used as a motivator for physical, security, and social needs: the debtor gains freedom from worry about bills, loss of job and income, being denied credit in the future, or having to pay additional interest and costs on this bill. Anxiety is a good motivator because so many aspects of being in debt are, in themselves, anxiety-provoking.

Earlier we discussed understanding people in debt — how and why they might have gotten into debt — in order to learn what motivations might influence them to get out of debt. The following examples illustrate ways of using this knowledge with different motivations and appeals to achieve Payment In Full.

PHYSICAL NEEDS

The first, most basic of our needs are our *physical needs*. These are primary to our existence and include food, shelter, rest, exercise, and health.

"Mrs. Jones, I understand your problem and I certainly want to work with you, but you do understand that failure to pay this bill could create a problem for you coming into this hospital/clinic/doctor's office at a later date."

This statement uses anxiety in its appeal to a physical need. Whether you mean that the doctor would not treat this patient again or mean that in the future this debtor would only be accepted on a cash basis is not relevant. All you are trying to do is make the debtor worry enough about her family's health care to pay the bill.

"Mr. Smith, you owe us for three months' rent. You wouldn't want to be in the position of not being accepted in another apartment because you hadn't paid this bill."

In some areas there are associations of landlords that circulate lists of people who skip out without paying their rent. The anxiety created by making sure that the debtor is aware of what could happen may be all that is needed to collect the debt.

You can remind a debtor that credit reputation is measured by the length of time it takes to pay a bill. The longer it takes him or her to pay a bill, the more reluctant creditors become in providing credit the next time it is needed. Since the bill is now overdue you must make it clear that it is to the debtor's advantage to pay it in the shortest possible time.

The following statements both appeal to physical needs and sound very similar. Think of the image created by each statement and you will see how the first uses pride in the motivation, and the second uses anxiety:

"You don't want to be denied credit because you did not pay this bill."

"You might be denied credit in an emergency situation."

SECURITY NEEDS

Second in importance (and most basic of our psychological needs) are our *security needs*. These are money in the bank, a job, the need to protect ourselves against threat and danger, whether real or imaginary.

A debtor may have money in a savings account, but will not withdraw it to pay the debt because of the "fear" of being without reserve funds. You may have to confront such a person with a greater security loss, such as that of not being able to obtain something he/she needs very much because no one will be willing to extend credit.

If you think the debtor might worry about losing his job (or missing a promotion) if his employer found out about the delinquency, you might ask him what he thinks would happen if his productivity at work dropped due to worry and frustration over this unpaid bill. What you can't do legally is actually inform the employer.

You could use a positive approach:

"Mrs. Jones, we know you want to take care of the problem so it won't be on your mind while you're trying to work."

Or a negative approach:

"Mrs. Jones, we certainly wouldn't want to have to sue you for this account, and then your employer might find out."

The statement above is legal if you are planning to do what you say you are going to do. As long as you are not actually threatening to tell the employer, then you don't have a problem. If the individual is sued and there is a public notice in the paper, you don't have any control over that.

For security needs, as with physical needs, anxiety is the logical appeal:

"You might be denied credit in an emergency situation."

"Your job will be more secure if you don't have the fear of having your wages put under garnishment." (If legal in your state.)

"You might end up having to pay additional interest and costs on the bill."

You've always had good credit in the past. I know you want to maintain that credit in the future so that when you need it, it's there for you."

Or security with pride:

"You don't want to be denied credit because of not paying this bill."

SOCIAL NEEDS

Next come *social needs*—association with other people, belonging, giving and receiving friendship and love. Debtors who are financially able to pay some of their bills react very strongly to social needs.

"What if your friends found out?"

"What if it was in the newspaper? People eventually find out things like this."

Most people are concerned with what other people think of them, and they are concerned what their family and their children and their friends would think if they found out. There is a very definite relationship between privacy and the social need. Good collectors are able to utilize the social needs, the interaction with people, the ability of the world to learn about the problems that the debtor is suffering.

These statements combine the social need with honesty as motivators:

"You have a good payment record with the creditor. You want to maintain that record."

"You want to do the right thing, don't you?"

These statements combine social needs with pride as motivators:

"You want to be thought of as an honest and reliable person."

"Your image is important to your future."

An appeal to social needs will probably not be the correct one for individuals who are distraught because of their condition —financial or medical—or their ability to make the payment is non-existent.

EGO NEEDS

Next are *ego needs*, which relate to self-esteem or reputation. Self-confidence, achievement, independence. Status, recognition, appreciation, and respect. We need to know that we have the ability to stand on our own feet and resolve a problem.

Most of the time, when debtors talk to you for the first time, they are ashamed about owing the money, and they need to restore a good opinion about themselves. They may say, "Yeah, I really do owe it but I've done everything I can to pay." Even though they may not have, they need to think that they have. Your job is to help them do that, to support them. You don't want to be in an adversary position; instead, you can help them do what you want them to do.

These statements combine pride and ego as motivators:

"You want to do the right thing, don't you?"

"To keep your self-respect, it is necessary to meet your obligations."

"You want to set a good example for your children."

"You don't want to be denied credit because of not paying this bill."

This statement combines anxiety and ego as motivators:

"How do you think your children will feel if they find out about the delinquent bills (or that their parent is a deadbeat)?"

These statements combine honesty and ego as motivators:

"It's right to pay, and it's wrong not to pay."

100

"You are a trustworthy person."

"You want to square yourself with the creditor and your own good conscience."

I know you are not looking to beat us."

"You have a good payment record with the creditor. You want to maintain that record."

"Your creditor extended credit to you in good faith." (The debtor, being an honest person, will want to show him-/herself worthy of the trust.)

"You will feel better knowing the debt is paid and you have done the right thing."

"You want to do the right thing, don't you?"

What would you do if your debtor said, "Oh, so you're calling about the bill we owe Doctor Brown. I understand your problem but I don't take care of that. My wife pays all the bills."

This response is obviously a stall. However, if it is true that his wife pays all the bills, then the debtor is facing an ego-bruising situation. This indicates that he will probably respond to the satisfaction of his ego needs. With pride and honesty as appeals, you could try this approach:

"Mr. Johnson, I can appreciate your not wanting to take care of the bookkeeping tasks in your household. But I am sure that as the breadwinner of your home, you make the decisions as to which bills are paid and which are not."

Or you could say:

"We know who really controls the pocketbook don't we, Mr. Johnson? We know that your wife writes out the checks, but you make the decisions, and I know that you want to make sure this is taken care of."

Then:

I know that you understand the seriousness of your delinquency. Remember, Mr. Johnson, that Dr. Brown waited as long as he could before attempting to get payment of this bill. The time to pay is now! Now, Mr. Johnson, would it be more convenient for you to have your wife write a check and mail it to us today, or would you rather stop by the office tomorrow?"

In this way you have reassured the debtor that he is: right in not doing the "menial task of bookkeeping"; the head of the household and the one who makes the decisions; an honest man in understanding his obligation; and that he must make a decision now! You follow this by giving him two minor alternatives from which to choose, either of which will provide payment.

Even if the man never looks at his wife's checkbook, he's never going to admit it. He's more likely to say, "Yeah, you're right, I do make the decisions in my family." And that's what you want him to say.

SELF-FULFILLMENT

When all the other needs have been satisfied, we seek *self-fulfillment*. This is the highest form of need. It is the need for realizing our potential, for continued development, for being creative. It can be as simple as setting a goal and achieving it.

"You will gain freedom from worry about this unpaid bill."

"You will like the security that comes from having squared away your debts."

Remember that we are all selfish people to some extent. We are interested in ourselves. Like everyone, debtors wish to maintain self-respect, self-acceptance, and self-preservation. In appealing to their needs, you have to find motivations to convince them that they will be better off paying the bill.

SALES APPROACH TO COLLECTIONS

The best way to combine motivation and effective communication in telephone collection is by thinking of it as a sales presentation. As you know, debtors usually find themselves in their present predicament because they are susceptible to sales psychology. Why not use this susceptibility to your advantage?

One of the key points in salesmanship is to *sell the benefit*. When selling a car, the salesperson sells the customer on the benefits of buying the car and not necessarily the car itself. He sells the comfort, the economy, the driving ease, and the prestige value. He mentions some of the benefits of having a particular motor, a type of upholstery, or certain mechanical gimmick that provides safety, speed, or whatever the buyer is seeking.

In the same way, you are selling the benefits of paying the bill — a good credit record, satisfaction of doing right, setting an example for the children, or investing to buy on credit at a future date. You must show what will be gained through that payment. Your job is to make the debtor want to pay the bill so badly that he just can't stand not to pay it! If you can generate this kind of reaction, you are using the right motivating factors.

MOTIVATING SENTENCES THAT COLLECT

1. You want to keep your credit good.
2. Show your good faith by paying the account today.
3. Some day you will need a good credit rating.
4. Your credit has been; don't damage it now.
5. Unless you do something, we must.
6. You will be amazed at what can happen if this account is not paid.
7. You must realize this can be controlled; why make it more costly.
8. You will save money by paying now.
9. Must we proceed without your cooperation?
10. We must do something; your action will determine what it is.
11. I know you face (or live up to) your responsibilities.
12. Would you rather deal with our attorney?
13. You won't find a collection to be as lenient as we have been.
14. We have only a limited time to collect this account. Pay it today or it may cost you more tomorrow.
15. Your credit rating (or record) can affect your employment record. You have a good job; why allow this account to affect it?
16. Is this amount really worth causing additional costs to be added to the account?
17. Someday your children could be affected by the credit reputation you are making today.
18. I have been both patient and fair with you. I expect you to pay me in full — immediately!
19. What would you do if you were in my situation? Wouldn't you want to get your money back?
20. There really shouldn't be any reason for me to take drastic action to recover money from a good customer like you.
21. I don't enjoy having to call you up for money, just as I am sure you don't like getting these calls. Let's clear up this business right now — today!

5. OVERCOMING OBJECTIONS

The letters PIF can stand for Payment In Full, or they can stand for Procrastination, Indifference, Failure. The effort you expend determines the result, and which definition will apply.

IF THE DEBTOR won't cooperate with you in finding a way to pay the bill, but gives you "reasons" for not paying, you have to be prepared to overcome his defenses, stalls, and objections, and motivate him to pay the bill. Practice will enable you to become skillful and at ease.

Your job is to make him feel that it is *necessary and will be pleasant* for him to pay what he owes, and that it will be *difficult and unpleasant* not to pay. You will convey enough urgency so that he understands that you are not going to let up if he has the ability to pay. You are going to show him that his resistance will be weakened, that you will get the money eventually.

As problems are brought up, listen closely and the debtors will tell you how you can motivate them to pay. For example, a man who mentions his family several times and how they should have the best of everything is giving you a clue that he can be motivated to "set a good example for his children" or "assure that he can provide them with what they need through maintaining good paying habits." The better you understand the persons you are confronting — their motives and frustrations, and how they react to these motives and frustrations — the easier it will be to tailor your approach for a successful collection.

It helps to remember that most debtors are anxious about being delinquent. They are fearful that something will happen to them if they don't do what they are supposed to do. When you call and identify yourself and why you are calling, you are making them more anxious and putting them on the defensive.

Therefore, besides telling you why they haven't paid, they are going to defend themselves. Their attitude may be argumentative or belligerent, they may try to blame someone else, they may plead with you, they may even try to flatter you. Nine times out of ten, these reactions are merely defensive. It helps if you recognize that.

On the other hand, to some debtors collecting is a game: who is going to get what out of whom? You are trying to get him to pay and he doesn't want to waste time with you on the phone. You want him to respond to your appeal to his needs. But you can't appeal to the need until you know what his objection to paying is. Therefore, you must find out the reason he hasn't paid the bill.

Many times the "reason" is really just a stall. A stall is not an objection to owing the debt or to paying it. What the debtor is saying, in effect, is, "I want to put this off." "I don't have the money right now." "I plan to spend it on something else." Or simply, "I don't want to face the problem." You have to provide reassurance that the problem *must be handled now* and that you are going to help him handle it.

Do not get discouraged when the debtor tells you the reason he feels that payment cannot be made. It gives you an opportunity to learn more about him. Here is where a thorough understanding of the nature and specifics of your business is necessary, or the debtor will have you at a great disadvantage. Most people who collect do not have this information, and here is where most collections are lost. Learning how to handle this type of conversation is what will make you an effective collector.

HANDLING THE CONVERSATION

When a debtor objects to paying the bill, one way you can handle it is by:

> Making a buffer type statement, then
> Turning the objection into a question,
> Answering the question, and
> Closing the sale once more.

For example, you've had acknowledgement from the debtor as to his identity and that the bill is owed. You made a trial close by asking whether the money will be mailed or brought to the office.

Mr. Debtor makes an objection: "I'm sorry, I just can't afford to pay that right now. I don't have the money."

Your buffer statement: "Mr. Debtor, I can understand why you would say that. There's a bottomless pit where money seems to go." (All you are trying to do here is soften the situation a little, so you can go on and stay in control of the conversation.)

Turning the objection into a question: "What you are really asking yourself is how important is the bill and can you afford to skip anything else to pay it? Isn't that right, Mr. Debtor?"

Answering the question (notice how the motivations are worked in): "Now I don't know about any other bills or any other purchases you are paying for, Mr. Debtor, but I do know that this bill is important to you. It was not paid as you agreed. As you know, future purchases on credit depend to a great extent on how quickly you handle your credit purchases of today. You really make your own credit reputation on how you pay. By paying this bill now you are avoiding a bad credit reputation. If a necessity arose to get your car fixed you could find the money. Well, this is a necessity in that it can affect your future credit.

Closing the sale: Mr. Debtor, will it be more convenient to send us a check today, or would you rather stop by our office tomorrow?"

Continue handling other objections in this manner until the debtor accepts one of the alternatives given, and you make your sale.

RESPONDING TO OBJECTIONS

To sell debtors on the idea of clearing the entire account today, you have to be able to deal with whatever excuse is presented. Debtors have many ways of saying they can't or don't want to pay their bills. Eventually you will hear what seems to be every excuse that could possibly exist. You will find, however, that these are all variations of a limited number of stalls and objections. With experience, you will learn successful ways of dealing with each type of excuse.

The following are common excuses used for not paying a bill—scenarios that all collectors face everyday—and some suggested responses and ways to handle them.

"Payment is in the mail."

"When was it sent?"

"Was it in cash or check?"

"What address did you send it to, and was it mailed to someone's attention?"

"How much was sent?"

"Was it the amount agreed upon? If not, why not?"

"Why didn't you pay on time?"

"It appears that the check has been lost. Will you mail us another one today (or come in)?"

Verify current information (address, employment, etc.).

Check if the due date coincides with debtor's paycheck.

"I'll send you a check."

Review debtor's promise record.

Verify how much money he is promising to pay, and when, and have him write it down.

Be sure he is able to keep this promise.
If you doubt him, ask where the money is coming from.
Don't accept promise beyond next payday.
Review with him what he has just promised.
Remind him of the date promised.

"They charged us too much."

"Why didn't you object at that time?"

"Why do you feel it is too much?"

"In what manner were you overcharged?" In valid disputes the debtor will have specific answers. In stalls his responses will be vague and non-specific. Challenge those types of responses by citing specifics to him, such as:

"Our prices are similar to others providing the same services."

"Our other customers/patients paying similar prices did not object." (If, indeed, the debtor's bill is higher than usual, be prepared to explain why; were there any special modifications, additional time, or extra service beyond that reflected on the bill?)

Promise to pay, that is broken.

"Why didn't you let me know?"

Remind him that the arrangements were a favor.

Tell him he didn't keep his word.

Don't agree to another promise until he understands this is the last one. No more favors will be given.

"We cannot pay right now."

"How soon should I look for payment?"

"When can you pay — will it be this month?" Don't leave this question open; let the debtor select a specific time slot and negotiate from that point.

"What seems to be the problem?" Asking this question may open a can of worms, but by utilizing proper control of the conversation you should be able to ascertain if the debtor has a real problem and often offer solutions to those problems.

"I'm not working now."

"Where were you working?"

"Why are you out of work?"

"How long have you been out of work?"

"Have you looked for work?"

"Are you on unemployment?"

"Are you receiving other income?" ("How are you living?")

"What are your prospects for work?"

"Why didn't you let me know?"

"Is your (spouse) working?"

"I don't have any money."

When will you get paid (or get your next check)?"

"What is the problem?"

"Do you mean you don't have the money right now?"

"I won't take food off my table to pay anybody."

"We are not asking you to do that. We are asking you to work with us in finding terms you can afford."

"I don't owe the account."

"Why?" This is one of the most effective collector replies. If the debtor's objection is valid, the steps needed to remove it from his name should be followed. Usually it is a dodge and the debtor is fabricating an alleged reason for non-payment.

"Why didn't you object when you received the bill?"

"My wife (or husband) and I are divorced (or separated)."

Get the date of decree or separation.

Get attorney's name for both parties.

Get employer's name for both parties.

Explain that their personal problems do not affect the fact that they owe the bill.

State that the responsibility is theirs and that you expect full payment *now*.

A divorce has little bearing on the liability of a debt incurred prior to the divorce. While laws vary from state to state, most contract law (the creditors' concern) centers on the parties agreeing to pay, not the parties named by another action to pay. A divorce decree will allow the parties to sue each other to enforce its terms, but generally it will not alter the rights of the creditor to collect from the responsible party.

"The TV never worked right."

"What do you mean by worked right?"
"Why didn't you object before now?"

Complaints about defective merchandise are common. The best reply is to center on the time factor. Find out what their dispute is, find out if they talked to anybody about it before, and get back to them. Stop the collection effort if you feel the dispute is legitimate.

"My insurance should have paid this."

"It hasn't, and we must look to you."
"Perhaps it will, but at this time we expect payment from you. You may follow up with your insurance company."

The fact of the matter is that your accepting an insurance third-party payment does not obviate their responsibility for the bill. Debtors will never understand that, they don't want to understand that. So that creates one of the constant problems.

Illness in family.

Ask who is ill. How does that affect the debtor's reason for not paying? Ask if this is an excuse for not paying.

If the debtor is ill, how long has he been out of work? When will he go back? Does he have disability insurance?

Find out if any financial assistance is being received from spouse, medical plan, or employer.

Why didn't he let you know?

Try for a definite promise.

Not home.

>   Find out who you are talking to.
>   Ask when debtor will be home.
>   Do not reveal purpose of your call unless it is to spouse.
>   Leave name (own name, not business name) and number.
>   If debtor is frequently not home when you call, consider that he is avoiding you.

Bankruptcy.

>   "Have you filed or are you just thinking about it?"
>   Ask for bankruptcy number and the court filed in.
>   Ask for name, address, and telephone number of attorney representing debtor.
>   Ask for name, address, and telephone number of the trustee.
>   Ask if your debt is listed in the petition and for how much.
>   Stop all collection efforts. The Federal Court is now involved.
>   File a proof of claim with the court.

Deceased.

>   Be understanding.
>   Ask for date and place of death.
>   Find out if there is an estate. Find out who is the administrator.
>   If there is no estate, ask about life insurance.

Bear in mind, during your conversations, that there are numbers of others who are trying to collect money from these people, too. They get inundated with creditors or credit companies calling them every five minutes about bills they owe, and you are just one of all those companies out there trying to get their money. So you have to show them why it is better to pay you than pay anybody else. The old adage that those who scream the loudest, the first, and the most are the ones who get paid is very true. But it's also the way you scream. You don't have to scream in a loud voice. You can motivate them to pay and lessen their resistance.

6. THE CLOSE

Make it easy for the debtor to say yes.
Have the debtor write down your address and
repeat it to you.
Review terms and dramatize importance of
keeping arrangement.
Review agreement and have debtor repeat, to
assure an understanding of what will be done
to pay the bill.

JUST AS A SALESPERSON is ready to close a sale whenever the buyer is ready to buy, you must do the same. Closing the collection sale can take place anytime during the interview — whenever you have obtained the goal of PIF or when acceptable terms have been agreed to. Listen. Not only will the debtors tell you how to motivate them to pay, they will also give you clues that they are ready to work with you to solve this problem.

Any of the following can be a clue that the debtor is ready to agree to pay:

"I don't want this on my record."

"My children come first."

"You will not call my employer."

"Will it be in the paper if I am sued?"

113

"Do I have to pay it in full?"

"I'm on a party line."

"This is my bill; don't call my wife (or husband)."

"I want to do the right thing."

At that point you may ask the debtor, "How much more time do you need to pay the balance due?" If he is properly motivated, he will be likely to agree with your suggestions rather than insist on a long payment term. Begin with PIF, if you believe there is any possibility for it, and work down from there to find an agreeable term arrangement. You might suggest (depending on what you think he can manage) one-half or one-third now and the balance at intervals to coincide with his paydays. Remember that his first offer will be lower than he can manage.

Get a committment for the amount, method, and date(s) for payment. Impress upon the debtor the importance of living up to his bargain. Ask him to write down your name, address, and what he has promised to do. Then have him repeat it to make sure that he thoroughly understands the agreement. You may want to send a follow-up note confirming the agreed-upon arrangements. Of course, you also will make a note of your phone conversation in his file.

For claims requiring long-term arrangements, determine what outstanding loans the debtor has and suggest that, when the loan balance is renewed, it include Payment In Full of the remaining debt. Place a flasher on the work card for followup.

Watch out for this trap: If the amount due on the last payment is very small, the debtor may not pay it because he believes you won't waste your time trying to get it.

When setting up terms, always be realistic about what the debtor is able to adhere to. Some retirees, for example, may want to pay the bill, but their bills add up to more than they can afford. What you want to arrange is something within their ability to pay, that allows them to keep their self-respect.

7. SAMPLE COLLECTION CALLS

THE PROCEDURE

1. IDENTIFY THE DEBTOR: Verify that you are speaking to the person responsible for the payment of the debt — the debtor or spouse. Verify the correct spelling of the name, and verify the address and place of business. In seeking the correct address, you might learn that the debtor has moved even through the phone number has remained the same. Be positive that you are speaking with the responsible party before you go any further in your call.

Debtor: Hello?

Collector: Am I speaking with Ms. Beverly Jones, the nurse, of 3930 NE 14th Avenue?

Debtor: Yes, this is she.

Collector: Your husband's name is Robert Jones and he works for Southern Associates?

2. IDENTIFY YOURSELF: Once you have confirmed that you are speaking with the right party and have the correct information, identify yourself by name and company.

Collector: This is Mrs. Harris at The Flower Shop.

3. ASK FOR FULL PAYMENT OF THE ACCOUNT: State your business firmly, but courteously. Let the debtor know that she must take care of this matter today; time is running out and she must act. You must impress upon her that the matter is urgent. Make her understand that payment must be made today, and in full.

> *Collector:* I need to speak with you concerning your account with The Flower Shop. This account was due at the end of the month and you are now seriously past due. We need for you to bring in a check for $57.18 today. However, we will accept your promise to mail us a check today in that amount.

The tone of your voice should clearly indicate to the debtor that she has no choice about making payment today, only that she may select which method she prefers.

4. UTILIZE A PSYCHOLOGICAL PAUSE: By asking the debtor for payment and then pausing, you leave the next move up to her. She will most likely give excuses about why the debt has not been paid and this should give you an indication as to which direction to take to get the account paid. A pause will usually make the debtor nervous. Let her make the move to break that silence. Don't make it easy for her.

5. FIND OUT WHAT THE PROBLEM IS: Listen carefully to the reasons she gives for not having paid the account and try to determine what the real problem is. You will find that if you let her do the talking, you will gain valuable information. There may be valid reasons why the account is past due, that can lead to your helping to solve the problem. You will probably get payment sooner if you can help her solve her special problem. Listen carefully to learn of any sources of funds that might be tapped to pay the account.

Debtor: I misplaced the bill and just forgot about it.

Debtor: I'm sorry that this has not been paid, but I had a
              lot of unexpected expenses this month.

6. *GIVE THE DEBTOR MOTIVATION TO PAY:* It's important to work with the debtor, but you must have control of the situation. No matter what the excuses are, she must be motivated to want to pay the bill. Be positive in your questioning so that every reply to you will be a "yes." Let her know that you assume that she will answer positively. Payment is taken for granted. Assist her in finding the best way to satisfy the debt.

Collector: Meeting your obligations is important to you. Am
               I correct, Ms. Jones?
Debtor: Of course. I have a responsible position in my job
               and I feel that I'm a responsible person.
Collector: I'm sure then that you understand that this bill is
               your responsibility, and that you do want to take
               care of it immediately.

Here you have appealed to her ego and her sense of honesty.

7. *DETERMINE A SOLUTION:* You may need to suggest ways that the debtor can get the funds to pay the account. Sometimes this can be a real challenge, as when husband and wife are divorced and neither accepts responsibility for payment of the debt.

8. *CLOSE:* Your aim is to collect the Payment In Full today and you and the debtor should agree on a method of payment. Suggest alternatives only after you find payment today is impossible. Impress the debtor with her responsibility. Make sure that she writes down not only your name and address, but whatever arrangements the two of you have agreed upon for payment. Be sure she understands the terms of your agreement. You, of

course, will make notes concerning the arrangements in the debt-or's file. In the event the debtor reneges on her promise, you will have a reminder of your conversation and be prepared to pursue the matter.

Collector: Ms. Jones, it is vital that you send me a check for the full amount and send it to me today. Please write this down.
Debtor: All right.
Collector: My name is Mrs. Harris at The Flower Shop. Our address is 4210 Main Street, Our Town, 00000. The amount due is $57.18. Will you please read that back to me?
Debtor: The Flower Shop, 4210 Main Street, Our Town, 00000. $57.18.
Collector: Will you mail us that check for $57.18 today?
Debtor: I'll try to.
Collector: Good. I look forward to receiving your check in tomorrow's mail. Goodbye.

USING MOTIVATIONS

APPEAL TO HONESTY

By playing on a person's honesty, you are reminding him of his desire to live by the rules of right and wrong. Most of us feel that to be honest is right and to be dishonest is wrong. An honorable person wants to do the right thing.

Most people believe themselves to be honest, and, therefore, right. Appeal to this belief can make you a successful collector.

Debtor: Hello.
Collector: Mr. Jenkins, Harold Jenkins, of 22 First Terrace?
Debtor: Correct. To whom am I speaking?

118

Collector: This is Mr. Smith of Acme Printing. I'm calling concerning your account with us. You have a bill here for $234.56 and it is seriously past due. We must have payment today. Would you like to come in to our office with the payment or do you want to put a check for $234.56 in the mail today?

Debtor: I certainly will not. The printing job was not right and I don't pay for poor work.

Collector: Mr. Jenkins, did you complain about the work at the time it was done?

Debtor: No, I guess not, but I am unhappy with the work and I won't pay for it.

Collector: Mr. Jenkins, you brought your printing job to us, correct?

Debtor: Yes, and you messed it up.

Collector: When you picked up the order, you agreed to make payment, correct?

Debtor: Well, you might not have given me the printing if I told you I wasn't going to pay for it.

Collector: Sir, we gave you credit in good faith. I am sorry that you are not satisfied with the printing. If you had complained at the time of delivery, we could have made corrections or adjustments for you. You do owe the bill and I'm sure that you want to live up to the agreement that we made when we gave you credit. You do want to continue to be trusted, don't you, Mr. Jenkins?

Debtor: Sure I do.

Collector: If you pay this account now, you will have no credit problems with us and I'm sure your sense of honesty will tell you that you have done the right thing. Now, which is easier for you, to bring a check for $243.56 to our office or to mail it to us today?

119

Debtor: I don't think I should have to pay, but as an honest man, I guess I'll mail you a check.

Collector: Mr. Jenkins, will you write down our address please?

Debtor: Yeah.

Collector: Send your check to Acme Printing, P.O. Box 450, Our Town, 00000, attention: Mr. Smith. The amount again is $243.56. Would you read that back to me?

Debtor: That's Acme Printing, P.O. Box 45021?

Collector: I'll expect your check in the next day or two. Thank you.

In this situation, the collector appealed to the debtor's honor. It was emphasized that the shop had trusted him with credit and he needed to show that the trust was not ill-placed. The collector overcame the debtor's unwillingness to pay by appealing to his sense of honesty. Probably, also, the printing was good enough to use or it would have been returned to the printer.

APPEAL TO EGO

People like to feel good about themselves and what they have accomplished. They want others to recognize them as worthwhile individuals. They want to be good role models for their children and to gain their respect. Collectors can use this as a motivation.

Debtor: Hello.

Collector: May I speak with Mr. James Fisher of 121 Front Street?

Debtor: This is he.

Collector: Mr. Fisher, I'm Mrs. Henry of Ace Tire Store. As I'm sure you know, you have a past due balance with us in the amount of $94.13. This is considerably past due and I must insist on getting a check from you today. Can you bring it in or will you put it in the mail today?

Debtor: Mrs. Henry, my wife is the only one in the family working, we have five children, and we are barely able to buy groceries, much less pay for the balance on these tires. I'll get to that bill when I can find a job.

Collector: I'm sorry about your unemployment, but this bill is very old and must be paid. How long have you been out of work?

Debtor: About two weeks.

Collector: Sir, you were employed when this charge occurred. Why didn't you pay for the tires then?

Debtor: We just couldn't afford to pay cash for the tires. I'll do my best to get it paid off soon.

Collector: Mr. Fisher, I'm sure your children know you don't have a job right now, but how would they feel if they knew you couldn't get credit anymore? What if someone was sick and you went to the drugstore to buy medicine and the pharmacist said that you couldn't have credit, how would you tell your children?

Debtor: That wouldn't really happen, would it?

Collector: You can ensure that it won't happen if you protect your credit by sending us a check today.

Debtor: I'll try. I'd feel terrible if my children knew I could not get them medicine when they needed it.

Collector: Thank you, Mr. Fisher. Will you be bringing your check to our store or can we expect it in the mail?

Debtor: I guess I'll mail it.

Collector: Sir, if you'll get a pen and paper, I'll give you the correct mailing address.

Here, the debtor was concerned not only that someone in the family might not get medicine if needed, but that his children might find out that he wasn't paying his bills. By appealing to his ego, the collector was promised—and received—the payment.

APPEAL TO ANXIETY

Some debtors don't seem to value honesty or even their ego, but they do respond to worry. They don't want to have unpaid bills hanging over their heads; they don't want to worry about what will happen if they don't pay them. They want the freedom from worry that comes with good credit. A good collector can appeal to a debtor's anxiety by convincing him that paying his bills will provide him with freedom from worry.

Debtor: Hello.

Collector: Is this John Jamison at 1520 Broad Street?

Debtor: Yeah, who's this?

Collector: This is Mrs. Jacobs at Downtown Appliance Store. As you are aware, your account balance of $437.58 is extremely past due. We must get the balance paid in full today. Would you bring a check for $437.58 to our store or can I expect it in tomorrow's mail.

Debtor: You've got to be kidding! I don't even *have* $437.58, much less to pay for a stove.

Collector: When you made a purchase of the stove, you also made the agreement to pay for it, didn't you?

Debtor: Well, sure. I don't think you would have given it to me as a gift.

Collector: You're right there. However, you made an agreement and we expect you to stick by it and send us the balance owed today.

Debtor: You can't expect it today. I've got lots of agreements to live up to.

Collector: Mr. Jamison, I know that you must be concerned about not paying your bills. I know that you realize how hard it is to build a good credit record again once it has gone bad. This is not only true of your credit record, but employers often take personal habits into account when considering ad-

	vancement in a job. If you don't pay us the amount owed today, we will be forced to take further action that could jeopardize more than just your credit rating.
Debtor:	Look, I'm not trying to get out of anything. I just have more bills than I can pay and I just can't pay them all.
Collector:	Mr. Jamison, do you belong to a credit union?
Debtor:	Well, yes, I do.
Collector:	Why don't you check with your credit union to see if you can take out a loan to pay off all your obligations and then only have one loan payment a month. Quite often, the payment on a consolidation loan is less than the combined payments on your outstanding debts are now. Are you willing to try it?
Debtor:	Yes, that might be a good idea.
Collector:	Fine. Call your credit union now and please get your check for $437.58 in the mail to us today. Do you have pen and paper to write down our address?
Debtor:	Yeah, I'll take it down.

When the appeal the honesty was not effective, the collector tried to instill worry in the debtor. The collector then had to help the debtor find a means for making payment. She knew from the debtor's original application that he belonged to a credit union, so she was able to use that approach to finding a solution.

In making a debtor worry, you must be careful not to violate any laws or the Fair Debt Collecton Practices Act. You are not allowed to threaten a debtor, however you can appeal to his anxieties without threatening him.

POSITIVE APPROACH

As you try to motivate debtors to pay, I think you'll find that most people react better to a positive attitude. If you let them know you assume that they are honorable people, they will act honorably.

Collector: I'm sure you want to assume control of your responsibilities, don't you, Mrs. Stone?
Debtor: Certainly.

Or, use this approach:

Collector: Mr. Ash, I'm sure you are pleased to be a good provider for your family, aren't you?
Debtor: Yes, I am.

The collector not only asked positive questions, but put the debtor in a position to answer affirmatively. Once the debtor is already agreeing with the collector, it makes it easier for him to agree again when asked for payment.

Collector: You are a person to be trusted, aren't you?
Debtor: Of course I am.
Collector: Then I know that you understand the importance of keeping your good credit with our office. I am sure that that is important to you.
Debtor: Yes, it is.
Collector: If you will send us a check today for the $50.00 balance, then you will maintain your good reputation with our office.
Debtor: OK. I guess I'll send you a check.

Another example:

Collector: You made a financial commitment to this store and I'm sure that you want to show yourself as someone to be trusted, is that correct?

Debtor: Yes, I certainly do.

Collector: If you pay this balance now, you will be OK with the store and with your own conscience. Now, will you bring your check to our store or will you mail it?

Debtor: I'll mail it.

If you take a negative attitude toward the debtors' interest in paying, you may anger them, which will make your job harder. Sometimes, however, you may get involved with a debtor who doesn't respond to a positive approach. He may be spurred on by negatives:

Collector: "Mr. Black, you don't want to be known as a person who doesn't pay his bills, do you?"

Understand, though, that a question such as this could anger the debtor or make him unduly defensive. You could lose the chance to collect. Usually the positive approach works best. With experience, you will know when to utilize the negative approach and with whom. Otherwise, deal positively!

DEALING WITH STALLERS

As you make calls, you will run across people who do not meet your expectation — they just plain won't pay. Don't lose your cool. Objections to paying, even from diehard non-payers, are usually just a means of buying time.

Debtor: I'm sure I paid that, I'll have to check.

Debtor: My wife told me that we didn't owe that amount.

Debtor: My husband handles paying all the bills. I just don't know. . . .

At this point the collector must affirm that the bill is indeed due and that the debtor has a responsibility to pay.

Debtor: Hello.

Collector: May I speak with Mrs. Clara Philips of 5 Midway Court?

Debtor: Yes, this is Mrs. Philips.

Collector: Mrs. Philips, is your husband still employed by the railroad?

Debtor: He is; who is calling?

Collector: I'm Mrs. Long, from Fieldings Department Store, calling about your unpaid balance with this store of $31.02. This account has been overdue for some time and must be paid today. Can we count on you putting a check in the mail for that amount today?

Debtor: I'm sure I paid this several months ago.

Collector: We have no record of receiving a payment on that account. We must have full payment immediately.

Debtor: I'll have to go through my cancelled checks to see if I paid that. Call me again next week.

Collector: I'm sorry, but this has gone unpaid for too long. We must have payment today. Please mail us your check immediately.

Debtor: Well, I guess I'll have to do that.

Collector: Let me give you our address. . . .

When the debtor said she would go through cancelled checks, the collector emphasized how urgent the matter was. The collector made it clear that payment had to be made that day and that she, the collector, would not be stalled.

DEALING WITH OBJECTIONS

There is a difference between stalling and objecting to paying. Objections frequently go along with a financial crunch. In this situation, try to determine the debtor's income and monthly expenses. Find out if he has any additional sources of income. If there was a credit application, there should be notations indicating savings accounts, credit union memership, etc. Involve the debtor in seeking a solution.

Debtor: I'm really in a bind. My bills are more than my income and I just can't see a way to pay them all.

Collector: Sir, does your place of employment offer credit union membership?

Debtor: Oh, yes, and I'm a member of the credit union.

Collector: Perhaps you could speak with the credit union manager and arrange for a consolidation loan. This would allow you to pay off your present obligations and probably have a lower monthly payment.

Debtor: That's a good idea. I hadn't thought about the credit union.

Collector: Then you will make arrangements with your credit union and mail us a check for $197.80 today?

Debtor: Yes, I'll make arrangements today.

Collector: Thank you, and have a nice day.

This is a typical objection: the debtor just doesn't have enough money to go around. When the collector suggested a solution that the debtor had not thought of, a successful collection was made.

The motivational appeals in these examples are very basic. In time, you will learn ways to modify them to suit different situations.

When you make collection calls, you must be sure that a way can be found to pay a past-due bill and then impart that belief to the debtor. If a debtor has more reasons to pay than not to pay, then collection will be much easier. You must help the debtor to find these reasons and then help the debtor to find the necessary funds.

So, follow the steps: identify the debtor, identify who you are and who you work for, give the reason for the call, ask for PIF, psychological pause, learn the reason for the delinquency, categorize by debtor type and why they haven't paid, classify what you anticipate the results of your discussion is going to be, close the deal. If you cannot close the deal at this point, find the right motivation and give him the right appeal.

I don't care if the bill is $10 or $10,000, the procedure doesn't change. Everybody reacts to stimuli. Your job is to find the stimuli, find the right motivation, find the thing that turns the key in his lock to get him to open his wallet.

Now go to it!

8. MISTAKES OF BEGINNING COLLECTORS

Professional collectors know that the objective of getting all the money will not be achieved all of the time, but also realize that if you never ask for it, you will never get it.

MOST NEW COLLECTORS encounter few, if any, problems through the first three steps: identify the debtor, identify yourself, state the reason for the call. From this point on, many have problems.

For example, it is impossible to know the next step to take in the call without knowing why the bill hasn't been paid.

Some find their collection call degenerating into an argument or a shouting contest when they attempt to motivate the debtor to pay the bill. Others have trouble in attempting to define the debtor's problem. Most find considerable difficulty when they try to find a solution for the debtor's problem.

Too often, the inexperienced collector will forget about motivation altogether, forget to give any explanation of the benefits of paying, forget to determine the debtor's problems. Then, rather than helping find a solution, the collector tries to impose a solution upon the debtor. It is this imposition of someone else's solution that results in all the fireworks — the final slapping down of the receiver and the preparation of yet another set of suit papers against the debtor.

If you should get flustered and lose your composition, as you realize that you are losing control of the conversation, give yourself a chance to start over. Say, "I am going to hang up now and I will call you back in fifteen minutes." This will give you an opportunity to review the debtor's file again and be better prepared.

Another problem comes up when the collector tries to motivate debtors into doing what the facts show that they are unable to do. This mistake can result in failure to collect forty to sixty percent of your accounts.

The experienced collector avoids these crises by putting more emphasis on attempting to understand debtors—attempting to interpret their responses—to determine their psychological position, and then letting them decide what they are going to do to pay the outstanding balance. The experienced collector has discovered that by guiding debtors and allowing them to solve their own problems, they are more likely to follow through and stick with the solution.

As you learn more about people and learn to judge debtors' responses with greater depth, you will have more to offer them in helping to solve their financial dilemma. That will help you become a better salesperson of those benefits.

PART IV

SELECTING A
PROFESSIONAL COLLECTION SERVICE

1. SELECTING A PROFESSIONAL COLLECTION SERVICE

Q. How do you choose a collection service?
A. Very carefully!

THERE IS A DIFFERENCE between first-party collection and third-party collection. This book is about first-party collection. You give credit, the individual defaults on the terms of that credit, and you try to find the money. If you can't get the money immediately, or show the individual how to pay, then you are going to have to do something else, which is refer the account to a third party, either an attorney or a collection agency.

Third-party collectors are people who are outside of the facility. They are impersonal. The attitude of the third-party collector is, "I'm not involved in what happens; I only know that this debt exists. If you don't have a legitimate reason for not paying, then we want the money."

Ethical conduct is as important as dollar results when a professional collector is servicing your accounts. It is especially important now, with the increased attention by government and courts to credit-collection practices. The collection service's methods of operation—its professional conduct and ethical practices—will reflect on *your* reputation, and can even possibly result in legal action against you.

In addition to the agency's ethics, unless it can produce results as far as your accounts are concerned, it is not the collector for you. This may be the time for your to review the service you are getting from your present collection specialist. Or, possibly, you are in need of one for the first time.

HOW TO BEGIN

Locate names of collection services by looking in the Yellow Pages of your telephone directory under "Collection Agencies." You should only consider those that list themselves as members of a trade association such as the American Collectors Association (ACA). Such membership is your guarantee that the agency has met a strict set of requirements, it is in full compliance with state laws, and that you have the backing of the facilities and staff of the association should any special problems arise. ACA, with a membership of approximately 2,600, is the world's largest organization of independent, bonded collection offices. Its members provide accounts receivable collection and other credit services for about 800,000 professional, retail, and wholesale credit grantors in 10,000 communities.

Ask for recommendations from other credit grantors. Find out which agencies have given them dollar results and ethical conduct. The type of service given other clients is a good indication of how your account will be handled.

Each time you contact a collection service, ask for references from clients in your own type of business and from their other clientele. Consider each reference in terms of whether it would expect the same level of performance that you would.

When you check the references, find out if the collection service brings good results and is prompt in settling for money collected. Ask if the staff is willing to give advice on credit- and collection-related matters when necessary.

Determine if the service has a good reputation in the community with merchants, professionals, hospitals, and other credit grantors. Find out if it has the good will and cooperation of local lawyers, the Better Business Bureau, and the Chamber of Commerce.

Visit the collection office. Often this will give you an indication of its professionalism. Find out if, in day-to-day practice, the operation is on the high level you want. Meet the staff. Note the office hours. And, of course, discuss all aspects of the collection operation and the services you will expect.

WHAT TO CHECK

The following guidelines are based on suggestions by ACA member Leonard G. Rose, president of National Account Systems, Inc., one of the largest collection services in the country.

ETHICAL OPERATION

Make sure there is compliance with your state's statutory requirements as to bond or license or both. Of the fifty states, thirty-one have such provisions. In addition, most states have controls for debt collection practices. You can get the information you need by contacting your state's commerce department or license division.

Collectors that belong to a trade association are expected to subscribe to and follow a code of ethics. There may be a statement of policy that employees are required to sign.

Ask for copies of all collection forms used in contacting debtors. Review them for Federal Trade Commission or Bar Association requirements. Watch for the use of simulated legal documents, which are contrary to FTC Guidelines.

FINANCIAL STABILITY AND COMPETENCE

Check the ownership and financial responsibility of the service. How long has it been in business? Investigate both the business and personal finances of management. They will be handling *your* money and you want to know *their* credit reputation.

Learn about the background and expertise of the staff. Does the manager and the staff keep up-to-date on new government regulations and court rulings relating to credit-collection practices? Are they up-to-date on the newest tools and techniques of collection? Check on the depth of management in case the manager or principal becomes ill or unable to perform his/her duties.

Review hiring practices. Is the service an equal opportunity employer?

SERVICES PROVIDED

Have a clear understanding of collection fees and what is and isn't included. Rates usually will be on a contingent fee basis: no collection, no charge. Be sure that all special situations are understood in advance; it may be desirable to have written confirmation to alleviate any costly misunderstandings.

Learn about the reporting practices. Are they computerized or manual? The service should give prompt acknowledgment of claims and it should return accounts judged to be uncollectible, without cost to you. It should notify you as to what investigation is being made on your claims, and if a payment has been made, that a check is coming.

Check the frequency of remittances (weekly, semi-monthly, or monthly) and the period covered. When sufficient volume is involved, you should be able to expect more frequent remittances to improve your cash flow.

Decide if the service is equipped to follow all accounts diligently for as long a period of time as required. Does it have complete and modern facilities for skiptracing? Is it computerized, so that it has instant access to the information on an account as well as its history, and is that information stored in the computer?

Ask about the geographic trade area that is covered, and if the service is able to forward accounts to a collection office in a location where a debtor may have moved. (One of the main reasons collection services join ACA is to be listed in the annual directory, which is used to forward 29 million dollars in accounts each year.)

Make it known that you expect your collector to exhaust all reasonable means toward securing voluntary settlement before recommending legal action. Be sure no legal action will be taken without your consent.

Ask about bonding of all employees and of coverage by errors and omissions insurance, which will protect you and the collection service in case of a lawsuit.

Ask how debtors are approached. Does it seem as though the collector will try to promote a sense of responsibility and emphasize the importance of a good credit reputation? Will the collector pay attention to your credit and public relations policies?

Determine if, because of the specific nature of your business, your particular needs can be met.

Base your selection on what you learn by discussing these topics, and on the company's reputation and past performance. Then you can be assured you have done everything possible to make a wise selection of a professional collection service. This is important, for such a service should be a profitable and compatible extension of your own credit operation.

PART V

COLLECTING WITHIN
GOVERNMENT GUIDELINES

1. WHY CREDIT GRANTORS
HAVE TO BE CAREFUL

THE CONSUMER SOCIETY is the single largest purchasing group in the United States, and its lobby groups in the state and federal congresses are among the most vociferous. Every time another consumer protection bill is passed, it erodes the abilities of credit grantors to regain the dollars lost through bad debts.

It is politically fashionable to vote in favor of consumer protection and consumer rights. Note, if you will, the bills before our state and federal congresses in election years, and you will find a marked increase in consumer protection bills.

The Annunzio Bill, commonly known as the "Fair Debt Collection Practices Act," (or "FDCPA") is witness to this consumerism concern on the part of our federal legislators. To be fair, the act is not intended to put the credit grantor at a disadvantage. It was intended to stop *unfair* debt collection practices and seems on its way to accomplishing this.

Many creditors must also comply with state laws that dictate debt collection practices. Some states have regulations more restrictive than the Fair Debt Collection Practices Act. Florida, for example, has become known as a debtor's haven because it regulates its creditors through what many of them have labeled the "little FTC bill," a law that embraces and expands the scope of the Fair Debt Collection Practices Act. No one is exempt, as the law is applied to "any person attempting to collect a debt."

There is no question that new laws have restricted some of your rights in collecting the monies owed to you. Nevertheless, there are still many legal ways for you to attempt to collect your money.

2. LEGAL USE OF TELEPHONE
FOR DEBT COLLECTION

THERE IS MUCH in the way of regulation that concerns the use of the telephone in debt collection. It is important to be aware and observe these policies and guidelines.

A number of years ago, Federal Communications Commission (FCC) outlined what it termed the *proper* use of the telephone, and it defined and regulated the *improper* use of the telephone for debt collection purposes. It was a punishable offense to abuse the use of the telephone.

The telephone companies helped disseminate this information by mailing to every telephone subscriber in the US a short flyer listing abuses of the use of the telephone, both as to reasonableness and frequency as prescribed by the FCC. As a result, a great cry arose because there was no explanation of what was meant by the terms used by the FCC.

FCC MEMORANDUM

When pressure was put on the FCC as a result, it issued a memorandum (November, 1970) on the use of the telephone for debt collection purposes. Its purpose was to answer certain recurring inquiries it was receiving concerning improper usage of interstate telephone service for the collection of claimed debts.

PUBLIC NOTICE
Federal Communications Commission
1919 M Street, NW - Washington, D.C. 20554

USE OF TELEPHONE
FOR DEBT COLLECTION PURPOSES

The Commission has received information that interstate telephone service is being increasingly used for collection of claimed debts in ways that are or may be in violation of applicable tariffs of the telephone companies and criminal statutes. Practices alleged include calling at odd hours of the day or night; repeated calls; calls to friends, neighbors, relatives, employers and children; calls making a variety of threats; calls asserting falsely that credit ratings will be hurt; calls falsely stating that legal process is about to be served; calls demanding payments for amounts not owed; calls to places of employment; and calls misrepresenting the terms and condition of existing or proposed contracts. Although many of these calls are placed on a local basis, there is increasing indication that such improper practices also involve use of interstate toll and Wide Area Telephone Service (WATS).

Tariffs of the telephone companies forbid use of the telephone "...for a call or calls, anonymous or otherwise, if in a manner reasonably to be expected to frighten, abuse, torment, or harass another;" or for calls that "...interfere unreasonably with the use of the service by one or more other customers;" or calls for "...unlawful purpose." Upon violation of any of these conditions the telephone company can, by written notice, discontinue service "forthwith." These tariff regulations are filed with this Commission pursuant to Section 203 of the Communications Act, 47 U.S.C. 203, and are binding on the telephone company and customer alike. Users of the telephone service are also subject to the enforcement proceedings provided for in Sections 401 and 411 of the Communications Act.

CALLS AT ODD HOURS

In general, any debt collection call is prohibited if it is placed at a time of the day or night that the calling party foresees would frighten, abuse, torment, or harass the called party (or any other person). The FCC explained that if, for example, the calling party knows that the called party works at night and sleeps during the daytime, then a call during the day would be in violation of the tariff, because the calling party could reasonably foresee that such a call would thereby harass, torment, abuse, or frighten the called party (or someone else).

Therefore, a telephone call at six o'clock in the morning or one made at eleven o'clock at night would not necessarily be a violation of the tariff. The issue, if one reads the memorandum correctly, is whether the time that has been selected for the telephone call would upset the called party.

REPEATED CALLS

The test is whether the calling party should reasonably expect or foresee that the effect of two or more debt collection calls would be harassing. A careful interpretation of the memorandum suggests that the FCC did not say that the placing of two or more phone calls within any period of time was a violation per se. The number of calls placed is not, in and of itself, the determining factor of telephone abuse, but rather the purpose of such calls.

CALLING PLACES OF EMPLOYMENT

Another question that has been posed is: What is wrong with calling places of employment about alleged debts owed by an employee? The answer depends upon the purpose, intent, or reasonably foreseeable effect of such calls. If the calling party calls the place of employment with the purpose, intent, or foreseeable effect of harassing, etc. the employer or employee or anyone else, such calls are prohibited. On the other hand, if reasonable efforts to contact a debtor at places other than at work have not been successful, then a call to the place of employment would not be objectionable if otherwise proper.

CALLS TO CHILDREN, FRIENDS, OR RELATIVES

The aforementioned test (that is, whether the calling party could reasonably foresee that the effect of a debt collection call will be harassing, etc.) also applies with equal force to debt collection calls made to children and friends, neighbors, relatives of alleged debtors. Moreover, there are serious questions concerning the possible breach of rights of privacy when debt collection calls are made to persons other than the alleged debtor. This adds a further dimension to the harassing nature of such calls, particularly if the claimed existence or nature of an alleged debt is discussed with persons other than the alleged debtor.

THREATS

With regard to making threats, asserting falsely that credit ratings will be hurt, falsely stating that legal process is about to be served, demanding payments for amounts not owed, or misrepresenting the terms and conditions of existing or proposed contracts, such calls are forbidden because the calling party should reasonably expect and foresee that they would frighten, abuse, torment, or harass the alleged debtor or someone else.

THE FAIR DEBT COLLECTION PRACTICES ACT

The following questions and answers regarding use of the phone under the FDCPA were prepared by the legal department of the ACA when the law was passed. Because of interpretation changes since then, and in the future, use this information as a guide only, and consult your attorney for actual interpretation.

I. Debtor Contact (Sec. 805)

A. *How often?*

Under the new law, there is no limit on the number of times a telephone collector may communicate with a debtor. However, the law does consider it a violation if a telephone collector "causes a telephone to ring or engages a debtor in telephone conversation *repeatedly or continuously with intent to annoy, abuse or harass any person at the called number."*

B. *When?*

Debtor contact should occur between 8 a.m. and 9 p.m. local time at the debtor's location. However, if the collector knows that this would be an inconvenient time for the debtor, the collector may not call between these hours. If the collector has the prior consent of the debtor or permission of the court, then he/she may call at times other than those specified. Note: The law is silent as to whether debtor consent has to be in writing.

C. *Where?*

The telephone collector may call at the debtor's home or his/her place of employment. However, if the collector knows, or has reason to know, that the employer (of the debtor) prohibits such communication, he/she may not call the debtor at the place of employment.

If the collector knows that the debtor is represented by an attorney on that particular account, then he/she must communicate with the attorney unless the attorney fails to respond within a reasonable period of time or consents to direct communication with the debtor. (ACA feels that 14 days is a reasonable time to wait to hear from the attorney.)

D. *Who?*

The debt collector may contact the debtor, debtor's spouse or attorney of the debtor (if this is known) as stated in C (above) when attempting to collect a debt. However, the collector may contact anyone after he/she receives a consent from the debtor (or debtor's attorney) to do so.

II. Validation of Debts (Sec. 809)

A. Within 5 days after initial communication with the debtor concerning an account, the collector shall then send the debtor a written notice containing the following, unless it is done in the original communication or payment is made within 5 days. Note: The notice can be printed right on the first collection notice. If the first contact is made by telephone and the debtor pays within 5 days, no verification notice is needed.

1. Amount of the debt.

2. Name of the creditor to whom debt is owed.

3. Notice that unless the debtor disputes the debt (or any portion of it) within 30 days, in writing, the debt will be assumed to be valid.

4. Notice that the collector will mail a copy of the verification of the debt or the judgment to the debtor if the debtor disputes the bill within 30 days in writing.

5. Notice that the collector will furnish the debtor the name of the original creditor, if it is different than the current creditor and the debtor contacts the collector within that 30-day period in writing.

B. If the debtor disputes the debt in writing, the collector must cease collection efforts until he/she furnishes the

debtor verification of the debt or a copy of the judgment
of the name of the original creditor, whichever may
apply.

C.   If the debtor fails to dispute the debt, this is not to be
construed by any court as admission of liability by that
debtor.

III. Multiple Debts (Sec. 819)

If a debtor owes multiple debts and makes a single payment, it
shall be applied according to the debtor's directions, if any,
and may not be applied to any debt that is disputed.

IV. Ceasing Communication (Sec. 805c)

If a debtor—or debtor's spouse, parent (if debtor is a minor),
guardian, executor, or administrator—notifies a collector in
writing that he/she refuses to pay or that the debtor wishes the
collector to cease further communication, the collector shall
not communicate further with the debtor except:

A.   To tell the debtor that he/she is terminating further efforts.

B.   To notify the debtor that he/she (or the creditor) may
take legal (or further) action.

C.   To notify the debtor that he/she (or the creditor) intends
to take legal (or further) action.

V. Harassment or Abuse (Sec. 806)

A collector may not engage in any conduct that tends to
harass, oppress or abuse any person in connection with the
collection of a debt. Although not limited to these, the following are prohibited:

A.   The use or threat of violence or other criminal means of
harming a person physically or through reputation or
property.

B. The use of obscene or profane language or that which will abuse the hearer or reader.

C. The publication of a list of debtors who refuse to pay except when sent to a credit reporting agency.

D. Advertising for sale any debt to coerce payment of the debt.

E. Causing a telephone to ring or engaging any person in telephone conversation repeatedly or continuously with intent to annoy, abuse, or harass at the called number.

F. Except when skiptracing, to place telephone calls without meaningful disclosure of the caller's identity.

VI. False or Misleading Representations (Sec. 807)

A collector may not use any false, deceptive, or misleading representation in connection with the collection of a debt. Although not limited to these, the following are prohibited:

A. The false representation that the collector is bonded (or vouched for) by the United States, or any state, including the use of a badge, uniform, or facsimilie thereof.

B. A false representation of:

    1. The character, amount or legal status of any debt;

    or

    2. Any services rendered or compensation that may be lawfully received by a collector for the collection of a debt.

C. The false representation or implication that any individual is an attorney or that any communication is from an attorney.

D. The representation that nonpayment of any debt will re-

150

sult in imprisonment or seizure, garnishment or sale of any property or wages of any person unless such action is lawful and the collector (or creditor client) intends to take such action.

E.   The threat to take any action that cannot be taken legally or that is not intended to be taken.

F.   The false representation or implication that the interest in the debt might be sold, referred, or transferred, and that such action may cause the debtor to lose claim or defense to payment of the debt or subject to any practice prohibited by the law.

G.   The false representation that the debtor committed any crime or other conduct in order to disgrace the debtor.

H.   Communicating or threatening to communicate to any person credit information that should be known to be false, including failure to communicate that a disputed debt is disputed.

I.   The use or distribution of any form or document that simulates or falsely represents that it is authorized, issued, or approved by any court, official or agency of the United States or any state, or which creates any false impression as to its source, authorization, or approval.

J.   The false representation or deceptive means used to collect or attempt to collect a debt or obtain information about a debtor.

K.   Except as provided under the Skiptracing section of the law (covered under "What a Skiptracer Should Know About the Debt Collection Practices Law"), the failure to disclose clearly in all communications to collect a debt or obtain information about a consumer (other than location information) that the collector is attempting to collect a debt and that information obtained will be used for that purpose.

L.   The false representation that the accounts have been turned over to innocent purchasers for value.

M.   The false representation or implication that documents are legal process.

N.   The use of any business, company, or organization name other than the true name of the collection service. It is ACA's position that the telephone collector can use his "business" or desk name or his personal name since the law is silent on the use of aliases.

O.   The false representation or implication that documents are not legal process forms or do not require action by the consumer (when in actual fact they are).

P.   The false representation or implication that a collector operates or is employed by a consumer reporting agency.

VII. Unfair Practices (Sec. 808)

A collector may not use unfair or unconscionable means to collect or to attempt to collect any debt. Although not limited to these, the following are prohibited:

A.   The collection on any amount (including any interest, fee, charge, or expense incidental to the principal obligation) unless such amount is expressly authorized by the agreement creating the debt or permitted by law.

B.   The acceptance by a collector from any person of a check (or other payment instrument) postdated by more than 5 days unless such person is notified in writing of the collector's intent to deposit such check (or instrument) not more than 10 nor less than 3 business days prior to such deposit.

C.   The solicitation of a postdated check (or other payment instrument) by a collector for the purpose of threatening or instituting criminal prosecution.

D. Depositing or threatening to deposit any postdated check (or other instruments) prior to the date on such check (or instrument).

E. Causing charges to be made to any person by concealing the true nature of a communication. Such charges include but are not limited to collect telephone calls and telegram fees.

F. Taking or threatening to take any nonjudicial action to dispossess or disable property if there is no right to possession of the property claimed as collateral through an enforceable security interest; or if there is no present intention to take possession of the property; or if the property is exempt by law from dispossession or disablement.

G. Communicating with a debtor regarding a debt by post card. Note: At the time of the writing of this handout, it was the opinion of one of the ACA negotiators that in the discussion with House and Senate (Subcommittee on Consumer Affairs) staff members that the use of postcards to request that a telephone number be called or that a person be contacted at a specific telephone number does not go against the intent of the prohibition of this paragraph.

H. Using any symbol or language other than the collection service's (or debt collector's) address on any envelope when communicating with the debtor by the mails or by telegram, except that you can use your business name if the name does not indicate that you are in the collection business. This does not prohibit the use of a company name that *does not* directly indicate that it is a collection service company nor does it prohibit the use of initials of the company followed by the address.

3. GENERAL QUESTIONS ANSWERED ABOUT THE FDCPA

THERE ARE MANY QUESTIONS that arise as collectors realize that they must collect in accordance with the federal Fair Debt Collection Practices Act (PL 95-109). (Those not covered under the law may still be subject to similar rules and interpretations of other agencies of the federal government, such as the FCC, Postal Service and/or individual state laws.)

The answers and explanations were prepared by the legal department of the ACA. Remember that this was an early interpretation of the law and that changes occur as the FTC makes interpretations or the courts make other decisions. For specific questions on the law, you should consult an attorney.

1. *Does the law cover commercial collections? (Sec. 803/5)*

No. The law only applies to debts contracted by consumers for personal, family or household purposes; it has no application to the collection of commercial accounts.

2. *Are credit grantors who collect their own debts covered by the law? (Sec. 803/6)*

Yes and no.

Yes: The law applies to credit grantors who collect their own debts using another name. Example: XYZ Department Store has a division called ABC Credit, which collects its accounts.

Therefore, the law applies to XYZ Department Store.

No: The law does *not* apply to credit grantors who collect their own debts under their own name.

3. *Banks and credit unions send certain past due accounts to other banks and credit unions for collection. Are they covered under the law? (Sec. 803/6)*

    The law applies to those activities of such banks and credit unions. However, other activities of those banks and credit unions would not be subject to the debt collection law.

4. *Recently the city of Boston published a list of citizens who did not pay their taxes. Is that forbidden under this law? (Sec. 803/6)*

    No. A governmental unit is not covered by this law. However, those persons whose names were published could possibly have a cause of action under invasion of privacy or impermissible publication statutes in that state.

5. *Is a consumer counseling service under the law? (Sec. 803/6)*

    No. Any non-profit organization performing bona fide consumer credit counseling services at the request of a consumer is not covered by the law.

6. *Are lawyers covered by the debt collection law? (Sec. 803/6)*

    No. An attorney-at-law collecting a debt as an attorney on behalf of and in the name of a client is not covered by this law.

7. *The law reads "Location Information" in Sec. 804, and not skiptracing. What is meant by location information? (Sec.803/7)*

    The definition section of the law states that "location information" means ". . . a consumer's place of abode and his telephone number at such place, or his place of employment."

8. *Is a collector allowed to call an employer of a debtor? (Sec. 804, 805)*

Yes and No.

Yes: When a collector is attempting to locate a debtor, he is allowed to communicate with the debtor's employer or any third party in such skiptracing efforts.

No: When a collector is attempting to collect a debt and wants to seek the help of the employer, he is not allowed to do so before judgment has been handed down.

9. *Is a collector allowed to ask the help of third parties as neighbors, friends and relatives in collecting a debt? (Sec. 804,805)*

No. The collector may not ask for their help *in actually collecting the debt.* However, he may seek their help when trying *to locate* a "skip."

10. *Is a collector allowed to make personal calls when attempting to locate a debtor? (Sec. 804)*

The law does not prohibit a collector from making personal calls in any skiptracing efforts.

11. *How often may a collector communicate with the employer of a debtor when skiptracing? (Sec. 804/3)*

Once, unless requested to do so again by the employer (or any third party). However, when the collector believes the information he obtained earlier from the employer (third party) was erroneous or incomplete and now this person has complete or correct information, the collector may communicate more than one time. (The bill does not say how many more times under these circumstances.)

12. *What about the use of postcards in debt collection? What does the law say? (Sec. 804/4)*

Postcards may not be used when attempting to collect, or collecting, a past due account. A collector may not use postcards in skiptracing efforts. In short, postcards are out.

13. *How often may a collector communicate with a debtor?*

There is no limit as to the number of times a collector may communicate with a debtor; however, Sec. 806 "Harrassment or Abuse" states that it is a violation of that section if a collector causes a telephone to ring or engages a debtor in telephone conversation *repeatedly or continuously* with intent to annoy, abuse, or harass any person at the called number.

14. *When may a collector contact a debtor? (Sec. 805a)*

Between 8 a.m. and 9 p.m. local time at the debtor's location. However, if the collector knows that this would be a time inconvenient to the debtor, the collector may not call between those hours. A collector, with the prior consent of the debtor, may call at times other than between 8 a.m. and 9 p.m. If a collector has permission of the court, he may also call at times other than between 8 a.m. and 9 p.m.

15. *What happens when a collector knows that an attorney is representing a debtor when the collector is attempting to collect from that debtor? (Sec. 805/a/2)*

The collector is not allowed to continue communicating with the debtor when the collector knows the debtor is represented by an attorney and knows or can easily ascertain the name and address of the attorney. However, if the attorney fails to respond in a reasonable (undefined in the bill) time, the collector may communicate with the debtor. If the attorney agrees to the collector communicating with the debtor, there is no problem. ACA feels that 14 days is a reasonable time to wait.

16. *Is a collector allowed to communicate with a debtor at the debtor's place of employment? (Sec. 805/3)*

Yes, *unless* the collector knows or has reason to know the

debtor's employer prohibits the debtor from receiving such communication at work.

17. *In attempting to collect a debt, is any communication permitted with the employer of a debtor other than in the skiptracing effort(s)? (Sec. 805b)*

First of all, a debtor may give his permission to contact his employer. Second, a collector may contact/communicate with an employer of a debtor after judgment has been handed down. Third, a court may give its permission to a collector to communicate with an employer before judgment. However, unless one of these conditions is met, no collection communication with an employer of a debtor is permitted.

18. *What happens when a debtor tells the collector he won't pay?*

Under Sec. 805c, "Ceasing Communication," a collector must cease communicating with a debtor when the debtor, in writing, notifies the collector that he refuses to pay or wishes the collector to cease further communication.

19. *If a collector must cease communicating with a debtor under the above conditions, what is the collector supposed to do? (Sec. 805c)*

The collector may then notify the debtor that legal action may be taken and where applicable, what that legal action will be. The past records of the collector must indicate that he does take the action he tells the debtor he intends to take.

20. *If a collector intends to take legal action, can he inform the debtor that he intends to take such action?*

Yes. A collector must actually intend to take the action he has "threatened to take" and his track record must show that he normally takes such action under those conditions. (Sec. 807/5, Sec. 805c/2-3)

21. *Is the word "harassment" defined in the law?*

No. However, the section on harassment and abuse (Sec. 806) lists a number of practices or procedures that are, under this law, defined to be harassment or abuse. A word of caution: in the same section, the lead paragraph states, "Without limiting the general application of the foregoing, the following conduct is a violation of this section." Which means that practices or procedures may be found to be harassment or abuse other than those six items listed.

22. *Some creditors post bad check lists in their stores; for example, grocery stores and gas stations. Is a collector allowed to post such a list of those who don't pay their bills?*

No. Such a practice would be harassment or abuse of a consumer or consumers so named under Section 806/3.

23. *May I pass on information regarding debtors to a credit bureau?*

Yes, under the provision of Section 806/3.

24. *Some of my competitors use forms with the word SUMMONS printed on them in bold type. Are these legal? (Sec. 807/9)*

No. Any form that simulates a document authorized, issued, or approved by any court, official, or agency of the United States is strictly illegal. There will be some problems in interpretation as to which forms are legal and which are not. *When in doubt, don't.*

25. *Is a collector required to disclose, in all his communications, that he is attempting to collect a debt? (Sec. 804, 807/11)*

A collector is required to disclose in all his communications with the debtor that he is attempting to collect a debt. In his skiptracing effort (Sec. 804) he is prohibited from making such disclosure when communicating with third parties.

26. *Does the law permit the use of an alias? (Sec. 807/14)*

160

The law is silent on the use of an alias by an individual collector. However, the law states that it is false and misleading to use any business, company or organization name other than the true name of the debt collector's business, company or organization.

27. *Is a collector allowed to add interest to a past due account he is attempting to collect? (Sec. 808/1)*

Yes, when the agreement creating the debt allows it *or* when it is permitted by law.

28. *I understand that postdated checks were prohibited in the earlier versions of the bill. What is the status of postdated checks in the final version as signed by the President? (Sec. 808/2)*

Postdated checks may be accepted by a debt collector. When a check is received that is postdated by more than 5 days, the collector must notify the debtor of the collector's intent to deposit such check not more than 10 nor less than 3 business days prior to such deposit.

One possibility collectors may consider is to accept checks with a current date and agree (with the debtor) to hold them until an agreed-upon date (or dates) when deposit would be made. To assure the debtor that this agreement would be followed, the collector could encourage the debtor to write on the bottom of the check or checks the agreed-upon date for deposit.

Under this section, a collector is prohibited from soliciting a postdated check for the purpose of threatening legal action. This section was included in the law after a debt collector used postdated checks for such a purpose, according to the House Subcommittee staff.

29. *Is a collector allowed to make collect telephone calls to a debtor regarding a debt collection matter?*

Section 808/5, Unfair Practices, states that it is an unfair practice for a collector to make such collect telephone calls when the true purpose of the call is concealed. The law does not prohibit such collect telephone calls when the collector clearly states the purpose of his call in that communication.

30. *If a collector addresses a postcard in the name of the debtor only asking him (debtor) to call the collector, is that legal? (Sec. 808/8)*

No, it is prohibited under the law to use a postcard in skiptracing efforts, and in collecting or in the attempt to collect from a debtor.

31. *Is garnishment permitted under this law?*

Yes, there is no change in the garnishment provisions of federal law under this act.

32. *Does the law prevent a collector from handling accounts that have been legally assigned to him in those states that permit the right of assignment, such as California?*

No.

33. *What does the Validation of Debt Section require of a debt collector under the law?*

Section 809 requires a collector to send the debtor a written notice within 5 days after the initial communication with the debtor in regard to a debt unless the debt is paid within that 5-day period. The written notice must contain the amount of the debt, the name of the creditor, a statement telling the debtor that the debt will be assumed to be valid unless the debtor writes and disputes the debt within 30 days, a statement that if the debtor writes within that time, the collector must obtain verification of the debt or a copy of the judgment and mail it to the debtor, another statement telling the debtor that within the 30-day period, the collector will send the debtor name and address of the original creditor if different from the current creditor.

34. *Does the collector have to stop his collection effort for 30 days after he sends that notification to the debtor? (Sec. 809b)*

No. The collector can continue his collection efforts until such time as the debtor notifies him of a dispute within that 30-day period.

35. *Can you use postcards in attempting to collect, forward, acknowledge forwarded accounts, or skiptracing? (Sec. 804/4, 807/11, 808/7)*

No. You may not use postcards if the information on them reveals that the recipient owes a past due account, or if any third party who reads the card can learn of a debtor's financial situation. This means postcards cannot be used to forward accounts nor acknowledge forwarded accounts as each must contain the name of the debtor, creditor, and amount.

It is also ACA's opinion that postcards cannot be used to attempt to collect past due accounts as they necessarily must ask for payment and identify both the creditor and the amount. In addition, it is ACA's opinion that postcards may not be used in skiptracing even though they contain only words similar to "Please call 555-926-6547."

This opinion is based upon Section 807/11, which requires a collector to disclose clearly in all communications made to collect a debt or to obtain information about a consumer that the collector is attempting to collect a debt or obtain information. Consequently, if a postcard containing only a telephone number were used, it would have to carry this disclosure and be a violation of the law.

36. *Can I use my company name on the outside of envelopes sent to the debtor while collecting, or sent to a third party while skiptracing? (Sec. 804/5, 807/11, 807/14, 808/8)*

ACA recommends that you use your company initials if your company name clearly discloses that you are in the debt collection business. If your company name leaves some doubt as to what business you are in, you may use it on return envelopes.

There are three sections of the law relating to this question. Section 804/5 states, "Any debt collector communicating with any person other than the consumer for the purpose of acquiring location information shall . . . not use any language or symbol on any envelope . . . that indicates that the debt collector is in the debt collection business."

Section 807/14 states that a debt collector may not use any false, deceptive or misleading representation . . . including . . . the use of any business, company, or organization name other than the *true* name of the collector's business, company or organization.

Section 808/8: "A debt collector may not . . . use any language or symbol other than the debt collector's address on any envelope . . . except that a debt collector may use his business name if such name does not indicate that he is in the debt collection business."

It is ACA's opinion that your initials are an abbreviation of your "true name" and acceptable on any envelope used for either collecting or skiptracing. You may also use only your address and omit your name entirely and be in compliance with these provisions in the law.

37. *May I use my company name on stationery used for letters to the debtor while collecting, or on letters to third parties while skiptracing? (Sec. 804/5, 807/11, 807/14, 808/8)*

You may use your company name on all collection letters addressed to a debtor as long as they are enclosed in envelopes.

It is ACA's opinion that you may also use your company name on stationery used for skiptracing even though your company name clearly reveals you are in the debt collection business, and that the letter is addressed to a third party, such as a former employer.

This might seem to be in conflict with a provision in the law (Sec. 804), which states, "Any debt collector communicating with any person other than the consumer . . . shall . . . not use any language or symbol...in the contents of any communication . . . that indicates the collector is in the debt collection business . . . ."

The purpose of this provision of the law is to avoid embarrassment; however, one of the principal intents of the law is to eliminate any deception. This is clearly spelled out in Section 802, "Findings and Purpose," which states: "There is abundant evidence of the use of . . . deceptive . . . debt collection practices . . . ." and, Section 807, which states: "A debt collector may not use any false, deceptive or misleading representation . . ." including "the use . . . of any written communication . . . which creates a false impression as to its source . . . ."

As the use of a name of a non-existent business would be in violation of one of the principal purposes of the law, just as would be sending a letter with no letterhead and carrying only the signature of the letter writer and his or her address, it is ACA's judgment that your company name, regardless of whether or not it can be interpreted to clearly reveal the nature of your business, can be used in the letterheads of skiptracing letters.

38. *In the last two or three years, the FTC has brought action against credit grantors as well as collectors because of lawsuits brought against debtors in courts in areas other than where the debtor is living. What does the new law say on this issue? (Sec. 811/2)*

The law follows the same line of reasoning the FTC did when it brought its action, which means that a collector must bring suit in one of two places: either where the debtor presently resides or where he signed the papers or agreement that created this debt.

39. *Is a collector prohibited from selling pre-collection letters or notices to creditors under this law? (Sec. 812)*

A collector is permitted to do so under the law unless such forms or letters indicate that someone other than the creditor is attempting to collect the bill when in fact this is not true.

40. *What are the penalties for violating this law? (Sec. 813a,b)*

Under the Civil Liability section, a collector is liable to an amount for actual damages as well as an additional amount, at the court's discretion, of up to $1,000. Under the class action provision, a collector is liable to an amount of up to $500,000 or 1 percent of the net worth of the collector if that is less than $500,000.

41. *When a collector has acted in good faith and yet inadvertently violated a section of the law, can he/she be held fully liable under the law? (Sec. 813c)*

There is a "good faith" clause under which a collector would not be held liable if it is shown that the violation was not intentional and resulted from a bona fide error. There is a further provision in the law which would not hold a collector liable when he follows the advice of the Federal Trade Commission under an Advisory Opinion.

42. *What is the time limit on bringing actions against a debt collector under this Act? (Sec. 813d)*

Any action brought under this law must be brought to an appropriate United States District Court within one year of the date on which the violation occurs.

43. *Who will enforce this law? (Sec. 814)*

The Federal Trade Commission is the enforcing agency and has the power and authority to enforce it under the Federal Trade Commission Act. A violation of this federal law will be deemed an unfair or deceptive act or practice in violation of the Act.

44. *The FTC is noted for its ability to write numerous rules and regulations on any area it enforces. Will this be done as far as this law is concerned?*

The FTC is expressly prohibited by Section 814d from writing trade regulation rules on debt collection that apply to debt collectors covered by this Act. The FTC still has the power to write rules and regulations for debt collection covering any others who collect debts but who are not covered by this Act, such as credit grantors in general.

45. *Does the new federal law apply to a state that has its own collection agency licensing act?*

The general intent of the law is to bring a general standard of debt collection practices throughout the USA. Section 816 of the law provides that a federal law would apply if that is stronger than the state law and, of course, in those states where there is no licensing law or debt collection regulatory law the federal law would apply across the board.

46. *If a state thinks its law is as strong or stronger than the federal law, is that state automatically exempt from the federal law?*

Sec. 817 provides that the Federal Trade Commission may exempt any state from the requirements of this law if that state has similar requirements and if there is adequate provision for enforcement by the state. This is similar to Truth-in-Lending provisions, which allow a state to be exempt if its Truth-in-Lending laws are similar to those of the federal Truth-in-Lending Act.

47. *When did the new law take effect? (Sec. 818)*

March 20, 1978, six months from date of enactment.

48. *Are there copies of the law available?*

Individual copies of the law may be requested from your Congressman. Up to three copies are available free of charge from the House Document Room, United States Capitol, Washington, DC 20515.

STANDARD COLLECTIONS OFFICE ABBREVIATIONS

Account	A/C	Beginning	Bg
Acknowledge,		Belligerent	Blg
Acknowledgement	Ack	Bill of Sale	B/S
Acknowledged	Ack'd	Broken Promise	B/P
Across	X	Brother	Bro
Across Street	A/St	Brother-in-Law	B/i/L
Additional	Addl	Business Address	B/A
Address	Add	Business Associate	B/As
Adjuster, Adjustment	Adj	Business Phone	B/Ph
Administrator	Adm	Business Reply	B/R
Advertising	Advg	Busy	By
Advise	Adv	Call Back, Called Back	C/B
Affidavit & Assignment	A & A	Called Debtor	C/D
Afternoon	P.M.	Called Employer	C/Emp
Agent	Agt	Cancel, Cancelled	Can
Agreement	Agrmt	Cancelled & Returned	C & R
Also known as	AKA	Can Pay	C/P
Amount	Amt	Cannot Locate	CNL
Another Payment	A/P	Cannot Pay	CNP
Answer	Ans	Certified Mail	Cert/M
Are	r	Changed, Charged	Chd
Arrange	Arr	Charged off	CH/O
Arrangements(s)	Argt	Chattel Mortgage	ChM
Assignment	Asmt	Check	Ck
Associate, Association	Asso	Checked	Ck'd
At	@	Checked with Neighbors	Ck/N
Attach, Attachment	Att	City Directory	C.D.
Attention	Attn	Claim	Clm
Attorney	Atty	Claims	Clms
Attorney Fee	A/F	Client	Cl
Auditor	Adtr	Collect, Collections	Col
Balance	Bal	Collect Call	CoCa
Bank	Bk	Come to Office	CTO
Bank Account	Bk A/C	Commission(s)	Comm
Bankrupt	Bkrt	Common Law	C/L
Bankruptcy	Bkcy	Compromise	Cmpr
Before	B/4	Conditional sales contract	CSC

Continue, Continuing	Cont	Each	Ea
Control Card	C/C	Each Month	EM
Convenient, Convenience	Conv	Each Week	EW
Correct Name	C/N	Employed	Emp
Court	Ct	Employer Notice	Emp/N
Court Costs	C.C.	Employment	Emp
Court Cost Credit	CCCr	Employment Inquiry	Emp/I
Court Costs Returned	CCR	Enclosed, Enclosure	Enc
Credit, Creditors	Cr	End of Month	EOM
Credit Bureau	CrB, CB	End of Week	EOW
Credit Guide, Yellow Book	Y/B	Envelope	Env
Credit Record	Cr/R	Evening	P.M.
Credit union	Cr/Un	Every Other Month	E/O/M
Criss Cross Directory	XXD	Every Other Week	E/O/W
Cross Filed	XF	Every Week	EW
Date of Last Charge	D/LCH	Execution	Ex
Date of Last Payment	D/LP	Exemption(s)	Expt
Daughter	Dau	Expense(s)	Exp
Deadbeat	D.B.	Extension	Ext
Debtor	Db or Dr	Extension of Time	Ext/T
Debtor Called	Db/C	Father	Fa
Decease, Deceased	Dec	Father-in-Law	F/i/L
Defendant	Def	File, Filed	F
Definite	Def	Final Demand	F/D
Definite Installment		Final Notice	F/N
Payments	Def/I/P	Forward	Fw
Delinquent	Dlq	Forwardee	Fwe
Dept. of Motor Vehicles	D/M/V	Forwarder	Fwr
Different, Difference	Diff	Forwarding Address	F/A
Direct	Dir	Forwarding Agent,	
Direct Payment	D/P	Forwarding Attorney	Fo/A
Disclosure	Disc	From	Fr
Disconnected	Disc	Garnishee, Garnishment	Garn
Dispute, Disputed	Dsp	Gave Report	G/Rpt
Disputed Account	Dsp/Ac	Give the Works	GTW
Divorce, Divorced	Div	Go Easy	GE
Does Not Answer	D/A	Going	Gg
Does Not Know	D/N/K	Guarantor	Guar
Do Not Compromise	DNC	Hard Luck Story	HLS
Do Not Sue	DNS	Has Receipt	H/Rcpt

He	H	Locate, Located	Loc
He Wrote	H/W	Long Distance	L/D
Home Address	HA	Long Distance Operator	L/D op.
Home Telephone Number	H/P#	Made Arrangements	M/A
Husband	Hsb	Maiden Name	Nee
In Care Of, Living With	C/O	Mail	Ml
Information	Info	Mailing	Mlg
Information Operator	Info/Op	Mail Returned	M/R
In Full	I/F	Make (or Making) Loan	Mk/Lo
In Jail	I/J	Make Arrangements	M/A
In penitentiary	I/P	Manager	Mgr
Installment(s)	Instl	Married	Mar'd
Insurance	Ins	Master File	M/F
Interest	Int	Maximum	Max.
Itemized statement	I/S	Merchandise	Mdse
Job	Jb	Minimum	Min.
Judgment	Jgt	Mother-in-Law	M/i/L
Laid Off	L/Off	Money Order	M/O
Landlord, Landlady	LL	Month	Mo
Large	Lg	Mother	Mo
Last Charge	L/Ch	Morning	A.M
Last Known Address	LKA	Mortgage	Mtg
Last Payment	L/P	Moved	Mvd
Left Blind Number	L/BN	Moved, Left No Address	M/LNA
Left Call	L/C	Nearby	N/By
Left Message	L/M	Nearby Phone	N/BYP
Left Name	L/N	Neglected	Negl
Left Name and Number	L/N&N	Negligent	Negl
Left No Address	L/N/A	Neighbor	Nb
Left Number	L/#	New Account	N/Acc't
Left Town	L/T	New Address	N/Add
Left Word	L/W	New Employment	N/E
Legal Action	L/A	Next Door	N/D
Legal Action Advised or		Next Month	Nx/Mo
Advisable	L/A Adv.	Next Week	Nx/Wk
Letter	Ltr	No Answer	N/A
License	Lic	No Credit Given	N/Cr/G
Line Busy	L/B	No Forwarding Address	N/FA
Liquidate(d)	Liq	No Good	NG
Living With, In Care of	C/o	No Money	N/M

No Record	N/R	Papers in File	Pa/Fi
No Service	N/S	Partial Payment	Par/P
No Small Payment	N/S/P	Past Due Payment	P/D/P
No Such Number	N/S/N	Patient	Pat
No Such Street	N/S/S	Payment	Pmt
Not Collectible	N/C	Payment Memo	P/M
Note	N	Payment Notice	P/N
No Telephone	N/F, N/P	Payment Plan	Pa/P
Not Home	N/H	Payment Refused	P/Rfd
Not In	N/I	Payroll Deduction	PR/D
Not in Criss Cross		Pensioned	Psd.
Directory	N/I/XX	Personal Call (outside)	P.C.
Not in City Directory	N/I/CD	Phone, Phoned	Ph
Not in Phone Book	N/I/PB	Phone Book	P/B
Not Listed	N/L	Phone Disconnected	Ph/Dsc
Not Our Party	N/O/P	Phoned Home	Ph/Ho
Not Working	N/W	Phoned job	Ph/J
Notice	Not.	Phone Not Listed	Ph/NL
Notice to Employer	N/T/E	Place of Business	P/O/B
Not Sufficient Funds	N/S/F	Plaintiff	Pl
Number	No.	Positive	Pos
Object, Objection, Objective	Obj.	Post Card	P/C
Office	Ofc	Postcard Appointment	P/CApp't
Old Account	O/Acc't	Post Dated Check	P/D/Ck
Old Address	O/Add	Pressured	Prsd
Old Employer	O/Emp	Prevent Further Action	P/F/A
On Vacation	O/V	Principal	Prin
Operator	Op	Profit and Loss	P&L
Operator's License	O/L	Promise(s) To Pay	P/T/P
Opposite, Opposed	Opp	Promise, Promises	Pr
Other Action	O/A	Promised Payment	P/P
Our Party	O/P	Promised Payment in Full	PP/F
Out of Business	O/O/B	Promises to come to office	Pr/C/O
Out of Town	O/O/T	Prompt payment	P/P
Out of Work	O/O/W	Put on pressure	P/O/P
Owns Own Home	O/O/H	Real estate	R/E
Paid	Pd	Receipt	Rct
Paid Direct	P/D	Receive, Received	Rec
Paid Direct in Full	P/DIF	Refer, Reference	Ref
Paid, Payment in Full	P/I/F	Refuses to Pay	R/T/P

Regarding	Re:	Statement	Stmt
Registered	Reg.	Statement Requested	Stmt/Req
Relative	Rel	Street	St
Rents	R	Street Guide	S/G
Report	Rpt	Subject, Substantial	Sub
Repossess(ed)	Repo	Substantial Payment	S/P
Request(s)	Req	Subterfuse	Gag
Request Client's Advice	R/C/A	Suit	Su
Request Report	Req/Rep	Suit Not Recommended	S/N/R
Response, Responsible	Rsp	Suit Notice	S/N
Responsible Party	Rsp/Pt	Summons	Sum
Return, Returned	Ret	Take up with Employer	T/U/E
Return Receipt	R/R	Talk, Talked	Ta
Return Receipt Requested	R/R/R	Talked on Job	Ta/J
Returned	Rtd	Telegram, Telegraphed	Telg
Returned Mail	R/M	Telephone, Telephoned	T
Salary	Sal	Telephone Book	T/B
Salesman	Slsm	Telephone Call	T/C
Same Address	S/Add	Telephone Directory	T/D
Same Old Story	S/O/S	Today	Tod
Self Employed	S/E	Tomorrow	Tmro
Semi-Monthly	S/M	Transfer, Transferred	Trf
Separate, Separated	Sep	Trick	Gag
Service, Services	Ser	Try to Borrow	T/B
Settlement in Full	S/I/F	Turn Over, Turned Over	T/O
Settlement Offer	S/O	Unable to Contact/Collect	U/T/C
She Wrote	S/W	Unable to Locate	U/T/L
Should Be	S/B	Unable to Pay	U/T/P
Sign, Signed	Sgn	Unclaimed	Uncl
Signature	Sig	Uncollectible	Unc
Signed Agreement	S/A	Unemployed	U/Emp
Single	Sgl	Unknown	Unk
Sister	Sis	Unpaid	Unp
Sister-in-Law	S/i/L	Unpublished Phone	
Skip, Skipped	Sk	Number	N/Pub
Small	Sm	Verbal	Vbr
Small Balance	S/B	Verified	Vfd
Soon as Possible	S/A/P	Verified Employment	Vfd/E
Special Letter	Sp/L	Verify	Vf
Starting	Stg	Wage Assignment	W/A

Week	Wk	Will Send	W/S
We Write	W/W	Willing to Pay	W/T/P
Wife	Wf	With	W/-
Will	W/-	Working	Wkg
Will Be In	W/B/I	Works	Wks
Will Call	W/C	Would	Wld
Will Call Back	W/C/B	Write, Written, Wrote	Wr
Will Come to Office	W/C/T/O	Yellow Book, Credit Guide	Y/B
Will Mail	W/M	Your	Yr
Will Not Pay	W/N/P		
Will Pay	W/P	$5.00 a week	5x1
Will Pay in Full	W/P/I/F	$5.00 each two weeks	5x2
Will Pay Part	W/P/P	$5.00 each three weeks	5x3
Will Phone	W/Ph		

174

Do you have everything you need for making effective collection calls?

The Collection Call is a 50-minute video cassette containing dramatizations that illustrate exactly how to make those all-important phone calls for collecting past-due accounts. Available in VHS and Beta.

ORDER FORM

To: Triad Publishing Company
1110 N.W. 8th Avenue
Gainesville, FL 32601

Please send me
_____ copies *The Collection Call* video @ $79.95 ea.
( ) VHS ( ) Beta
_____ copies *Payment In Full* @ $24.95 ea.
_____ sets *Payment In Full* and *The Collection Call*
@ $95 per set ( ) VHS ( ) Beta

Name _____
Address _____
City/State/Zip _____

All orders are shipped promply. Please enclose check for exact amount, adding $2.50 for postage and handling. Please include 5% sales tax for orders sent to Florida addresses. Foreign orders payable in US funds drawn on a US bank. Prices subject to change without notice.